Literature and Social Med

From Instapoetry to BookTube, contemporary literary cultures and practices are increasingly intertwined with social media. In this lively and wide-ranging study, Bronwen Thomas explores how social media provides new ways of connecting with and rediscovering established literary works and authors while also facilitating the emergence of unique and distinctive forms of creative expression. The book takes a 360° approach to the subject, combining analysis of current forms and practices with an examination of how social media fosters ongoing collaborative discourse amongst both informal and formal literary networks, and demonstrating how the participatory practices of social media have the potential to radically transform how literature is produced, shared and circulated. The first study of its kind to focus specifically on social media, *Literature and Social Media* provides a timely and engaging account of the state of the art, while interrogating the rhetoric that so often accompanies discussion of the 'new' in this context.

Bronwen Thomas is Professor of English and New Media at Bournemouth University and the author of *Narrative: The Basics* (2016).

Literature and Contemporary Thought

Literature and Contemporary Thought is an interdisciplinary series providing new perspectives and cutting edge thought on the study of Literature and topics such as Animal Studies, Disability Studies and Digital Humanities. Each title includes chapters on:

- why the topic is relevant, interesting and important at this moment and how it relates to contemporary debates
- the background of and a brief introduction to the particular area of study the book is intended to cover
- when this area of study became relevant to literature, how the relationship between the two areas was initially perceived and how it evolved

Edited by Ursula Heise and Guillermina De Ferrari this series will be invaluable to students and academics alike as they approach the interdisciplinary study of Literature.

Available in this series:

Literature and Social Media

Bronwen Thomas

 Routledge
Taylor & Francis Group

LONDON AND NEW YORK

First published 2020
by Routledge
2 Park Square, Milton Park, Abingdon, Oxon OX14 4RN

and by Routledge
52 Vanderbilt Avenue, New York, NY 10017

Routledge is an imprint of the Taylor & Francis Group, an informa business

British Library Cataloguing in Publication Data
A catalogue record for this book is available from the British Library

Library of Congress Cataloging-in-Publication Data
Names: Thomas, Bronwen, author.
Title: Literature and social media / Bronwen Thomas.
Description: London ; New York : Routledge, 2020. |
Series: Literature and contemporary thought | Includes bibliographical
   references and index.
Identifiers: LCCN 2019044602 | ISBN 9780415789035 (hardback) |
   ISBN 9780415789097 (paperback) | ISBN 9781315207025 (ebook)
Subjects: LCSH: Hypertext literature–History and criticism. |
   Literature and technology. | Literature and the Internet. | Books
   and reading–Technological innovations. | Online authorship.
Classification: LCC PN56.I64 T53 2020 | DDC 802.85–dc23
LC record available at https://lccn.loc.gov/2019044602

ISBN: 978-0-415-78903-5 (hbk)
ISBN: 978-0-415-78909-7 (pbk)
ISBN: 978-1-315-20702-5 (ebk)

Typeset in Sabon
by Taylor & Francis Books

Contents

Figures

Note

While some theorists complain that the term 'social media' too often elides differences between platforms, I will use the term to refer to the general phenomenon, but will refer to Twitter, Facebook etc. when I am making specific points about the affordances and contexts of use of distinct platforms, apps and services. Following common practice, I will also use social media in both the singular and the plural depending on the sense of the sentence. I fully expect that during the course of the publication of this book changes to the ownership, terms and conditions and even the very existence of some of the platforms discussed will occur, so I apologise in advance for any apparent inaccuracies. Terms appearing in bold are briefly explained and referenced as appropriate in the glossary.

Acknowledgements

This book would not have come about without Jon Bish's championing of Twitter which gradually wore down my resistance, and Chindu Sreedharan's enthusiastic embrace of the platform as an outlet for creativity and play. My thanks, too, to Zara Dinnen and Ed Finn for their comments on the original proposal and to the series editors, Ursula and Guillermina for their feedback on the first draft.

I am grateful to the Faculty of Media and Communication at Bournemouth University for an award supporting a short period of research leave which allowed me to start work on this book. Thanks, too, to friends and colleagues from SHARP, ISSN and PALA who have sat through many of the conference papers where I explored some of the initial ideas behind the study, and to the followers of @onlinereaders1 who have entertained and taught me so much over the years.

Special thanks to the following who have granted permission for me to use direct quotations from them:

@Joannechocolat; @arjunbasu; @HooklandGuide; @chaletfan; @MicroFlashFic; @Trakl_Bot; @MagicRealismBot; @angelreadman; @sorayabakhbakhi.

Thanks also to @terriblytiny for putting me in touch with their authors and to Jenai Dalal and Divyanshi Vyas for permission to quote from their work. I am grateful to Professor Wesley Raabe for permission to quote from correspondence in Chapter 2, and to Tim Wright for allowing me to interview him regarding his experiences with Unbound.

Some material from Chapter 3 has previously appeared in *Comparative Critical Studies* Issue 13.3 (2016), Tales from the Timeline: Experiments with Narrative on Twitter. Reproduced with permission of The Licensor through PLSclear.

Series Editors' Preface

Since the turn of the millennium, literary and cultural studies have been transformed less by new overarching theoretical paradigms than by the emergence a multitude of innovative subfields. These emergent research areas explore the relationship between literature and new media technologies, seek to establish innovative bridges to disciplines ranging from medicine, cognitive science, social psychology to biology and ecology, and develop new quantitative or computer-based research methodologies. In the process, they rethink crucial concepts such as affect, indigeneity, gender, and postcolonialism and propose new perspectives on aesthetics, narrative, poetics, and visuality.

Literature and Contemporary Thought seeks to capture such research at the cutting edge of literary and cultural studies. The volumes in this series explore both how new approaches are reshaping literary criticism and theory, and how research in literary and cultural studies opens out to transform other disciplines and research areas. They seek to make new literary research available, intelligible, and usable to scholars and students across academic disciplines and to the broader public beyond the university interested in innovative approaches to art and culture across different historical periods and geographical regions.

Literature and Contemporary Thought highlights new kinds of scholarship in the literary and cultural humanities that are relevant and important to public debates, and seeks to translate their interdisciplinary analyses and theories into useful tools for such thought and discussion.

Ursula K. Heise and Guillermina De Ferrari

Introduction

Why 'literature' and 'social media' are not antithetical

Social media is often associated with the 'Shallows' (Carr 2010), and the worst excesses of triviality, ephemerality and narcissism. Meanwhile, literature is celebrated for its ability to challenge norms and assumptions, to elevate the trivial, and to provide insights into universal aspects of the human condition that transcend the here and now. It may even be defined as relying on a process of 'consecration' (Bourdieu 1983: 320) of the kind associated with a religious object of devotion. Nevertheless, this study will argue that, building on the networking opportunities and seemingly low barriers to participation of the world wide web (Jenkins 2009), social media **platforms** such as Twitter, Facebook, Instagram and Tumblr have offered spaces for the production and dissemination of innovative creative works, as well as radically transforming modes of engagement with those works. Some of these developments can be associated more broadly with 'post-press literature', which is 'created outside of the established circles of book production' and which engages with the 'new possibilities for economic and artistic agency that arise at the intersections of the literary field and digital culture' (Levey 2016). However, the study will also focus on the unique ways in which social media becomes embedded in the user's everyday activities and facilitates linking and 'spreading' across media (Jenkins, Ford and Green 2013). While I will seek to explore continuities with existing literary forms and traditions, I will argue that social media is having a profound impact not just in terms of the production and consumption of individual works by individual writers and readers, but also with regard to the cultural intermediaries and industries 'working at the intersection of culture and economy' (Matthews and Smith Maguire 2014: 1) that both surround and shape what comes to be defined as literature. My study will therefore approach the subject of the literary not just in relation to texts or works but taking into account processes of production and consumption, the roles of networks and movements, and industrial and institutional contexts.

As the following sections outline in more depth, the study draws on terms and concepts from a wide range of scholarly and non-scholarly sources and fields, and aims to provide in-depth analysis of, and critical reflection on, contemporary literary practices, activities and institutions as they appear on the social media platforms so many of us have incorporated into our daily routines. However, a defining feature of the study will be its approach to literary value as 'already always implicated in commercial systems' (Bode 2012: 102) and its enthusiasm for the ways in which emerging practices challenge the hegemony of many existing routes to and modes of literary engagement.

The rise of social media and key issues/critiques

The second decade of the twenty-first century has seen a backlash against cyberutopianism, with concerns about privacy, monetisation, bullying and a growing realisation that far from expanding horizons, social media may offer little more than **echo chambers** where the same views and voices endlessly circulate. Likewise, critics such as Fuchs (2013: 102) have called for an increased focus on the role of social media within the political economy, to examine whether **convergence** and the seeming democratisation of the media associated with network cultures mainly benefit global corporations rather than powerless individuals, resulting in what he calls the 'corporate colonisation of social media'. The term 'data colonialism' (Couldry and Mejias 2018) has been coined to highlight the ways in which the so-called data revolution relies on normalising the exploitation of human beings whose work in maintaining the systems and structures we rely on is often unseen. It is also used to challenge the marginalisation and exclusion of speakers of languages other than English.

Meanwhile, the rise of social media has coincided with concerns about precarity and a shift towards short term contracts and a 'gig economy' where flexibility of work practices is gained at the expense often of fundamental safeguards. Particularly at risk here are those working in the creative industries where the powerful ideology of 'passionate work' (McRobbie 2016: 36) is used to present low paid and precarious work as thrilling and desirable to those who would seek to position themselves as 'creative'. Concerns have also been raised by commentators, theorists and artists (e.g. Carpenter 2018) about the environmental fallout from the pressing need to store vast quantities of data, often impacting on the land or seascape and disrupting habitats.

In 2017/18 the activities of Cambridge Analytica, a data analysis firm based in the UK, led to increased debate about the potential political influence of data mining, with Facebook in particular being accused of helping to harvest data and promulgate 'fake news' with consequences for key political events, including the UK Brexit referendum and the US Presidential elections. In the wake of the Cambridge Analytica scandal, many commentators have expressed concern about the 'territorialising' (Fülöp 2019) tendencies of large multinationals, particularly their evasion of tax and legal obligations to the nations they use as bases for their operations. Even the apparently technical and neutral concept of the platform has come under scrutiny (Madrigal 2019), exposing the idea that all providers are doing is providing a platform for the free expression of content as nothing more than an 'excuse' for evading the same kind of responsibility for publishing content that broadcasters and the press are faced with.

The rise of social media has been explored against the backdrop of neoliberalism, particularly with regards to the foregrounding and privileging of the first person (Marwick 2013), but also in relation to the kinds of sociality they promote. As Hungerford (2016) has noted, this has led to greater reflexivity about what we mean by 'the social', influenced by Latour and **Actor Network Theory** and the idea that 'social connections only deserve the name when they are acted upon, that the social only exists at all when its networks are activated' (Hungerford 2016: 4). Similarly, theorists have begun to more closely scrutinise key concepts such as 'connectivity' (van Dijck 2013) and 'sharing' (John 2016) which are widely used by social media platforms as a way of maximising monetisation and exploitation of users.

The idea of online spaces and social media sites as places where networking and dissemination of content may be subject to commercial forces sits uneasily alongside concepts such as that of the 'gift economy' operating in particular in fan communities, where users not only freely share content but their time and labour in maintaining those communities. When we add to this the often uncomfortable relationship between commerce, culture and the literary, and the emergence of sites that seem to be specifically set up to allow creative producers to charge consumers for accessing content, it is perhaps easy to understand why so many may feel disillusioned and sceptical. In Chapter 6 I will discuss how certain online writing communities such as Wattpad have moved towards creating paywalls for content and hierarchies amongst users. On YouTube, 'Super Chat' replaced Fan Funding as a means to allow viewers to directly pay content producers, while on Tumblr users can commission others to produce bespoke content. Meanwhile sites such as Kickstarter and Patreon provide further vehicles for creative producers to generate income – in some cases to make the production possible, but in others to provide a steady source of revenue once the product has been launched.

Concerns about the psychological and emotional impact of social media have focused on younger or more vulnerable users. Particular attention has been paid to so-called toxic practices and behaviours online, including hate speech and direct threats of violence. Whether social media simply reflects or amplifies these views and behaviours remains a matter of debate. But for the authors of titles such as *Ten Arguments for Deleting Your Social Media Accounts Right Now* (Lanier 2018), the focus on the sensational and the negative that drives traffic and engagement results in nothing less than a 'toxic miasma of bad vibes' (O'Connell 2018).

Nevertheless, a 'growing tiredness over the "exploitation" thesis' (Lovink and Rasch 2013: 15) has led to the exploration of alternatives to social media monopolies, and practical ways in which users can demonstrate their freedom and resistance (Williams 2018). As a result, studies of social media set out to go beyond and behind what is visible on these platforms, to focus on architecture, infrastructure and close analysis of how they are being engaged with and shaped by users. For Livingstone, whose research focuses in particular on children and the media, rather than blame users for their lack of media literacy skills, we should instead try to ensure that we create a 'digital environment that treats ordinary people more fairly and equitably' (2018: 9) and to acknowledge the experiences of users who are frustrated, distrustful and resistant.

Technology and literature

While it might be the case that 'Technology is a key defining factor in twentieth-century culture' (Goody 2011), advances in technology have also long been perceived as a direct threat to literary cultures, associated as they often are with the mechanistic and the industrial. In his theory of **uncreative writing** (discussed in more depth in Chapter 5), Goldsmith (2011) overturns conventional wisdom to make a virtue of the ways in which recent technologies have exacerbated mechanistic tendencies in writing and to fundamentally challenge traditional notions of the creative genius and the canon. However, regardless of whether we see technology as a force for good or evil, it is indisputable it helps make visible many of the processes and relationships that contribute to the production, circulation and consumption of literature. As well as unprecedented levels of access to authors, publishers and critics, the world wide web and social media provide us with huge amounts of data and metadata relating to readers and reading, providing potentially valuable insights into the creative process and the formation of literary tastes and preferences. Social media platforms, with their distinct **affordances** and diverse practices, allow us to observe the multiplicity of ways in which those engaged in literary activities both express themselves and express their appreciation, admiration or criticism of the creations of others, incorporating text, oral responses, images and sometimes a combination of different modalities and channels of communication.

'Electronic literature' (discussed further in Chapter 1), embracing works created by or for computers but also those that rely on new media and digital networks for their distribution, has radically unsettled existing definitions and understandings of the literary, by means of both artistic and theoretical exploration. In particular, electronic literature shifts the focus from the surface of writing (Wardrip-Fruin 2006) to the wider process that contributes to the production and dissemination of that text. While many forms of electronic literature rely on 'extensive and deep tacit knowledge' (Hayles 2008: 4) of existing literary tropes and conventions, they often call into question fundamental literary terms and concepts, in particular around ideas of authorship, character and plot. They also necessitate analysis and discussion which are sensitive to multimodality and the specific affordances of electronic texts.

Chapter 1 will outline in more depth the nature and scope of these redefinitions and challenges, but I will argue that there are important continuities and discontinuities between the kinds of literary experimentation, play and participation of 'electronic literature' and those we find emerging on social media platforms. A key difference, for example, is the simple fact that social media has only really been able to take hold thanks to a dramatic leap in technology: people are now able to carry around with them smartphones that are much more powerful and sophisticated than the desktop computers on which the earliest examples of 'electronic literature' were produced.

Chapter 1 will also set out how discussion and analysis of electronic or digital literature has itself gone through different phases or 'waves' (Bell, Ensslin and Rustad 2014) and relies more and more on dialogue between the disciplines of literary criticism, media and cultural studies. Early studies of '**born digital**' literature tended to rely on binary oppositions between print or analogue forms and the digital, and in their concentration on form and describing the impact of new technologies, fell into the trap of **technological determinism**. However, even today there is often a tendency to overstatement, generalisation and determinism. For example, in their introduction to a volume of essays on *The Digital Critic: Literary Culture Online*, the editors assert that 'Digital culture is currently changing every aspect of literature' (Barekat, Barry and Winters 2017: 11), even though they go on to concede that 'Not everyone in the literary world is enthused by digital technology' (12).

In *Television: Technology and Cultural Form* (1974), Raymond Williams provided an influential critique of technological determinism and the assumption that technology causes change rather than being part of a complex combination of social, economic and cultural forces. Equally, Williams reminds us that the adoption of new technologies may be uneven, and that the uses to which they are put can be highly unpredictable. More recently, Standage has warned of the perils of 'chronocentricity' (2000: 199) whereby we neglect the fact that what we take to be unique about our generation is little more than a reprise of previous historical moments. And **New Materialism** and Actor Network Theory have pointed to the ways in which nonhuman as well as human 'actants' help shape culture, rejecting both technological and social determinism in favour of a focus on relations and mutual influence (discussed further in Chapters 4 and 5).

Key theoretical approaches and influences

This study will examine the variety of forms of creative expression we can find across social media, as well as the myriad ways in which readers, followers and users respond to, curate and adapt literary texts. As Murray (2018: 20) argues, here 'literature to a large extent becomes what the digital literary sphere *deems* to be literature'. Influenced by 'recently reenergized' (Murray 2018: 17) literary sociological approaches to the hidden or forgotten producers of contemporary literary cultures (e.g. English 2005; Squires 2007), the discussion will include analysis of how literary texts and their authors are marketed and branded via social media, online literary festivals and prizes, and online literary communities. It will also consider how the study of literature has changed in the light of new computational approaches and the vast amounts of data digital devices and platforms make available. This 360° approach reflects the ways in which digital and online cultures have made it more difficult to sustain divisions and boundaries between modes of production and consumption, and between material that is conceived of as existing outside or inside of a stable core literary artefact. The study is therefore not just concerned with trying to identify and define the kinds of literary expression emerging from social media, but also to understand how people and institutions, organisations and industries use social media as a space where the literary can be celebrated, shared, reviewed, curated, marketed and sold. In this respect, I share with Hungerford (2016) a desire to connect with those 'unknown participants' who collaborate to bring into being new or existing literary worlds, though part of my argument will be that social media makes this collaboration and work highly visible in new ways.

My approach is also informed by social practice theory and its insights into how media are 'embedded in the interlocking fabric of social and cultural life' (Couldry 2006: 47), particularly how social media give us stories that 'cross over into our daily lives' (Walker 2004:1). Related to this is a problematizing of divisions between consumption and production, work and leisure in the new political economy of the digital age, where seemingly routine or everyday activities may result in the production and circulation of cultural texts or artefacts, and where 'ordinary' people from their living rooms or workplaces may act as **cultural intermediaries**, or '**influencers**' shaping notions of taste and cultural value. I will therefore approach the 'field' of literature in the Bourdieusian (1993) sense by focusing on the practices of a whole range of individuals, organisations and institutions that are positioned by but also help reproduce social and cultural hierarchies and symbolic or cultural capital. While this concept of field is useful for suggesting the ways in which we can move beyond traditional literary criticism's focus on text, it is especially useful with regards to social media because it provides a challenge to more consensual views of social life and illuminates the 'mechanisms of value and power that structure the literary field' (Weber 2018: 22). Murray (2018) has questioned Bourdieu's relevance to 'de-territorialized' online domains where the cultural brokers may no longer be individual or even human. Nevertheless, Bourdieu's theories remain influential in making those forms of brokerage more transparent, and in demonstrating how notions of value and taste purporting to come from a position of economic disinterestedness so often in fact are driven by commercial and class interest.

At the same time, while my interest in literature and social media has been prompted in large part by a desire to engage with the vast amounts of material easily available to researchers and to everyday readers, I will explore how far works on social media can be discoverable and recognisable as literary, without the trappings (book covers, retail environments, established cultural intermediaries) that help us make these distinctions when it comes to print works. In addition, I will consider whether the sheer amount of data available online makes it more difficult to draw boundaries around the literary as something removed from and distinct from the everyday or the popular. In this respect, my approach is informed by traditions derived in particular from cultural studies that theorise the 'everyday' and the 'ordinary' as 'repeated practices that organise a daily flow' for cultural life, but also as spaces where resistance and subversion become possible (Morris and Murray 2018: 10). My interest in social media platforms therefore derives from the ways in which they act as 'vectors for the production, transmission and interactions of culture' (Morris and Murray 2018: 3).

Studies of digital literature (e.g. Hammond 2016; Murray 2018) often characterise the digital in broad terms as an 'age' or 'sphere' from within which the literary needs to be investigated anew. However, this is the first study to specifically address the impact of social media and to examine in depth the kinds of literary activity and audiences that have emerged from these spaces. My approach to the topic is heavily influenced by studies which have examined how contemporary literary culture is being trans-formed and redefined by social and cultural changes that necessitate a consideration of how literature interacts with and exists alongside popular visual media, and is being enjoyed, shared and critiqued with others in open social contexts as never before (Collins 2010). Such work moves from close reading of texts to examining what surrounds cultural texts, whether this is magazine interviews with authors, television book clubs, film adaptations or advertisements and publicity materials.

Collins' study is provocatively subtitled 'How Literary Culture Became Popular Culture' and sets out to explore both how reading and literature have been absorbed into popular media and how notions of literary taste have come to be perceived as more easily accessible. An important context for Collins' study is the emergence of Amazon into a retail landscape where books were already being routinely sold alongside other media content in mega mall stores, and where a culture of amateur reviewing has become firmly established. Alongside increasing scrutiny of the roles of cultural intermediaries such as online book retailers, the publishing industry itself has been forced to examine its own record in terms of encouraging diversity, with the emergence of initiatives such as The Good Literary Agency (https://www.thegoodliteraryagency.org) which aims to increase diversity in the publishing industry.

The study of literature as an increasingly contested category thus looks beyond the traditional confines of the discipline to engage with previously castigated or marginalised activities and practices, including marketing and promotional materials, adaptations and cross-media fertilisation. For exam-ple, Jagoda's *Network Aesthetics* (2016) combines an analysis of literary representations of the network with the pop cultural (film, tv and **ARGs**) to try to understand how the concept of the network both defines but is defined by users, particularly in the context of **participatory cultures.**

In media and cultural studies, renewed interest in paratextual material (Gray 2010) relating to contemporary cultural texts has prompted discus-sion and debate of the cultural value of materials and activities previously dismissed or marginalised as belonging to the realms of the commercial. This work expands Genette's (1997) concept of the **paratext,** originally developed in relation to literary texts, to refer to the kinds of materials (blurbs, prefaces, commentaries) that may provide an important 'threshold' to the interpretation of that text, but which have tended to be neglected as being separate from, or outside the text. Docherty (2014) has argued that such is the interest in paratextual materials, that they now appear to be 'hogging the spotlight' to the neglect of the 'star attraction' or the 'good stuff' to which they relate. He goes on to associate interest in the paratextual with the idea of 'distracting digital clutter' in general. Docherty claims that this is largely an approach confined to the fields of economics, technology and sociology rather than the humanities with its 'residual disciplinary affinities' that 'privilege the text as the holy of holies'. However, literary scholars engaged with the study of multimodal literature (Gibbons 2012) or the intersections between the literary and the digital (McCracken 2013) are also returning to Genette and the idea of the paratext. The idea that we need to look beyond the confines of a single text to embrace discussion of context and audience is certainly at the centre of my 360° approach to the topic of this study, particularly as so many of the texts I discuss are distributed across media, produced collaboratively and often require content creators to be highly skilled in promoting their work.

Such work necessitates engagement with media and cultural theory, especially theories relating to participatory cultures (Jenkins 2009) and active audiences (Fiske 1987). Moreover, it requires at least a basic understanding of technological change, for example the role of **algorithms** in predicting tastes and purchases. It also requires understanding how wider cultural shifts, such as that towards on-demand provision of content from the likes of **Netflix**, come to shape and define user expectations and experiences in all sorts of other fields, including that of literature.

Another key influence in this regard is the field of internet studies, and particularly the emergence of '**platform studies**' which aims to 'promote the investigation of underlying computing systems and how they enable, constrain, shape and support the creative work that is done on them' (https://mitpress.mit.edu/books/series/platform-studies). In the case of my study, it means engaging with changes of use, updates to terms and conditions and user responses, while of course recognising that these may be subject to further revision and even complete removal of services at any point.

An interest in materiality and material cultures also defines the contribution of book history in foregrounding both continuities and disruptions with previous cultural shifts affecting access to and enjoyment of literary works. For example, Murray's work on an emergent digital literary sphere (2018) attempts to build bridges between literary studies, the **digital humanities** and book history and industry practice. With the work of Bourdieu providing the main theoretical framework for her study, Murray sets out to interrogate the boundaries between what she sees as a text-centric humanities and the contextual social sciences, while at the same time engaging with methods from the emerging field of the digital humanities. In so doing, her aim is to combine analysis of textual matter with analysis of the wider institutional and cultural context for the literary.

Murray's study provides a challenge to scholars from these disciplines both to engage with emergent practices and platforms and to take them seriously, and to look outside their own disciplines for theoretical and methodological insights. Murray acknowledges that her study is rooted in book history, and largely leaves discussion of 'screen studies' until the end. Her main point of reference in terms of the lineage for the digital literary is electronic literature, and she is cautious about including popular fiction and **fanfiction**, though she does discuss young adult fiction. Like her previous groundbreaking study of the adaptation industry (Murray 2012), *The Digital Literary Sphere* provides important insights into the infrastructures and political economy of the business of literature in the digital age, for example the working practices and corporate values of Amazon, and the commercial imperatives guiding publishers and festivals in the digital age.

My approach differs from Murray's in being more focused on user-generated content and the interactions and collaborations between users/readers and producers/authors that the digital facilitates. While Murray's book provides insights into the industry contexts for the emergence of digital literary works, my study relies more on observation of and immersion in the communities and spaces where creative expression is circulated, shared and discussed. In addition, my focus on literary outputs generated on social media, often incorporating multimodal elements and responding to the specific affordances of different platforms, addresses McNulty's (2018) call for critics of digital literature to 'learn to look, in a new way, beyond the printed book'. While I will be concerned with analysing and critiquing the practices of users and readers in the context of wider questions of reading formations and interpretive communities, and analysing the affordances of different platforms and infrastructures, I am less concerned with trying to map or define the contours of the digital literary landscape or 'sphere'.

While this study breaks new ground in focusing on social media as a space where literary cultures and works can flourish, work on storytelling in social media from the narratological and linguistic fields provides an important context for understanding how the '**small stories**' (Georgakopolou 2007; Page 2010) of social media circulate, gain influence and create impact. In particular, Mäkelä (2019) has drawn on research on the 'allegedly unsophisticated material' (160) of social media updates to draw parallels with literary techniques and strategies such as simultaneous narration in the novel. Mäkelä contends that it is possible to look beyond traditional literary genres for examples of the 'literary' by adopting a stance or strategy 'characterized by a heightened attentiveness to the creativity of form, ambiguity, and the exchange between intentional artistry and accidental aesthetics' (161). While this offers an important assertion of the contribution that models and approaches from the fields of literature, narratology and sociolinguistics provide in helping to map and critique literariness beyond the traditional boundaries, the focus remains predominantly on narrative, language and form, making it less able to account for the ways in which the works are disseminated and shared by users, or how they incorporate multiple modalities and media.

In the course of this study I will consider the various ways in which access to social media may be restricted, for example due to issues with device-specific operating systems, or for reasons of cost, geography, age or other 'participation gaps'. I will for reasons of practicality mainly examine English language usage of social media, and the reach of my study is inevitably delimited by my own sphere of interests, **social networks** and social practices. Nevertheless, I will include some discussion of regions where the mobile phone has become a major conduit for literary exchange, particularly China and Japan.

My study seeks to avoid some of the alarmist rhetoric of many discussions, for example Hammond's (2016) *Literature in the Digital Age* which opens by asking 'Is literature dying in the digital age?'. It also seeks to avoid the tendency of studies lamenting the seeming demise of print cultures to rely on simplistic binaries, and inclines towards optimism rather than pessimism in its approach to the changes to literary culture and practice experienced since the advent of social media.

Forms of social media

A working definition offered by the editors of *The Sage Handbook for Social Media* is that it refers to 'those digital platforms, services and **apps** built around the convergence of content sharing, public communication, and interpersonal connection' (Burgess, Marwick and Poell 2017). These can be dated back to the mid to late 1990s and to sites such as Six Degrees (1996) which introduced profiles, friends and lists influencing the development of Facebook and My Space some years later. Theorists of social media have focused more and more on examining in depth the infrastructures of specific platforms, digging down into their practices, terms and conditions and mission statements. In addition, van Dijck (2013) has argued that the focus needs to shift to how these platforms shape and define new practices and forms of sociality, and to interrogate how seemingly free content and social spaces are in fact dependent on delivering users in huge quantities to marketers and global corporations. Van Dijck has been influential in calling for theorists to debunk some of the prevailing and powerful myths around social media usage, particularly how notions such as 'connectivity' can be a mask for commercial exploitation. As the study of social media becomes more established, engagement with the technology has become more of a focus, as theorists become adept not only at understanding how bots or algorithms work, but also at using the tools for gathering data that social media facilitates.

Van Dijck's (2013) typology of social media helps to provide a basic insight into the different form and functions of existing and emerging platforms and services. While she accepts that the distinction between these types is not fixed, breaking down social media in this way can be helpful as a first step to mapping how and where social media forms arise and how they relate to one another:

1   Social networking sites, e.g. Facebook and Twitter, based on establishing and maintaining interpersonal contact between individuals, but relying only on very weak social ties
2   User generated content, e.g. YouTube or Flickr, allowing for the sharing of media content from multiple devices.
3   Trading/marketing sites, e.g. Amazon, ebay.
4   Play/games oriented sites, e.g. Farmville.

The study of social media as a subdiscipline of internet studies particularly addresses the need to document and interrogate the history of technologies, platforms and user behaviour. Two of its most influential theorists, Nancy Baym and Jean Burgess, have been collaborating on producing a 'biography' of Twitter as part of their contribution to the 'second wave' of platform studies, incorporating critical thinking about the roles platforms play in mediating contemporary communication and cultural environments, and integrating materialist approaches from software studies into its methods (Baym et al. 2016).

Meanwhile Papacharissi and Easton (2013) argue that it is possible to approach different social media platforms as distinct examples of the Bourdieusian habitus, with their own normative, ingrained behaviours and notions of taste developed through contact with others with similar backgrounds or life experiences. Nevertheless, Papacharissi and Easton also extend Bourdieu's notion to what they call the 'habitus of the new' across social media, identifying commonalities around the expression and storying of the self and the importance of connecting with others.

Following these approaches, in the sections that follow I provide a brief overview of some of the most well-known and popular forms of social media, reflecting on their history but also their main features and affordances as at the time of writing.

Twitter

Twitter, the microblogging platform which restricts users to posts of no more than 280 characters (140 until 2017), dominates discussion of social media, perhaps because it has become so influential in setting up and maintaining academic social and professional networks. Although its mission statement is constantly being updated, in February 2016 it defined its main function as 'To give everyone the power to share ideas and information instantly, without barriers' while the importance of story-telling was signalled by the main web page banner, inviting users to 'tell your stories here'. In all its iterations, the emphasis is on 'real-time updates' and the present tense and directive speech acts feature heavily, drawing users in and inviting participation. Users have to sign up to the service and set up an account. They can then follow the accounts of other users and be followed in turn, and **tweets** posted by followers will appear in their timeline with the most recent tweets appearing first. Various clients (e.g. TweetDeck, Twitterific) exist offering users different **interfaces** and facilities. Many users will not only rotate between these clients, but will access tweets via different devices, making it difficult to generalise about the user experience and the makeup of individual timelines.

Twitter will be prominent in the discussions that follow (especially Chapter 3), having given rise to its own literary forms (Twitterfiction), and being one of the main conduits for interaction between authors and their readers. Twitter was set up in 2006, according to Rogers (2013: x) primarily as an urban lifestyle tool for users to keep others updated about their activities. Its origins and history have been covered in depth elsewhere. Here, I note two important aspects of its evolution as a platform. The first is that many of the features that define Twitter today were introduced or heavily influenced by users, for example the hashtag (used primarily to signal participation in a shared topic) and the retweet (sharing someone else's tweet with one's followers). The second is the amount of data Twitter makes readily available to users in terms of trending topics, how many followers a user has at any one time, how many times their tweets are **liked** or **retweeted** and so on. In its short life, Twitter has undergone a number of key and sometimes controversial changes (see for example van Dijck 2013; Weller et al. 2013). Some of these can be difficult to track, but the company's own statements in the

'About' section of the website have gone from direct address (What are you doing?) to the more general and abstract (What's happening in the world and what are people talking about right now?). This reflects how its reach and claim to be able to influence events has grown, but also how its main form of communication is based on the idea of addressing potentially large groups of people as each tweet reaches not just everyone who is **following** a particular account, but also their followers, making it impossible to fully know or control one's audience.

Accessing Twitter usually means rejoining the timeline where the user last left off, but it is up to users whether they begin reading at that point or scroll up to the most recent tweet and work their way backwards. Users can like/favourite tweets and retweet posts to followers, allowing them both to manage content and contribute to its distribution. Another way they can do this is by using **hashtags** to start up conversations and create trending topics, or by replying to and quoting tweets. Though Twitter is mainly about sharing text, the facility exists to link to images and videos from within the 280 characters. While tweets rapidly disappear from most users' busy timelines, they can be archived and retrieved by various means, or collated and preserved by means of lists or screenshots. In early 2016 changes to the service, including removing the cap on the length of tweets, resulted in an outcry from users, horrified at the prospect that many of the features people once found confusing and restrictive but which had now become affectionately familiar could soon disappear. In November, 2017 a new 280 limit was introduced, and although some users responded by saying that they preferred to continue to restrict themselves to 140, as time has progressed discussion around the limit has gradually diminished.

Facebook

Facebook is often associated with the worst excesses of the **attention economy**, with users attempting to manage their profiles to display themselves in the most flattering light, and to accrue followers and likes like commodities. It suffered significant reputational damage in the aftermath of the Cambridge Analytica story and interference in US and UK domestic politics. The history of Facebook's creation in 2004 has been mythologised in the film *The Social Network* (2010), adapted from *The Accidental Billionaires*, written by Mezrich in 2009. In June 2017 Facebook achieved a new milestone, reaching two billion monthly active users, compared to Twitter's 328 million. Like Twitter, Facebook has had major overhauls, notably the Timeline feature introduced in 2011, which changed the default profile from a list of recent updates to a complete timeline of the user's major life events since birth (usually based around school, college, marriage), all worked out by an algorithm, based on the idea of helping users to create more 'complete' profiles. The change was just one of many which raised questions about users' privacy and seemed to demonstrate how powerful a hold these platforms can have over users' content, contacts and even their sense of self. Facebook for many is synonymous with social media, and the main way in which they share content, connect with others and keep up with the latest news. However, it will feature less prominently in my discussion; although it is used widely for discussion around the business of literature and for promoting authors or titles, I have found far less evidence of Facebook being used as a platform for creative expression than is the case with Twitter.

Tumblr

Tumblr, set up in 2007, is 'so easy to use that it's hard to explain', but is mainly associated with blogging and the communities that arise around particular interests and tastes. As originally conceived by founder David Karp, Tumblr was attractive to many users for its seeming protections of privacy and the fact that it purported to rely neither on the selling of ad space nor of user data (Munteanu 2017). Although the takeover by Yahoo (itself shortly afterwards taken over by Verizon) was controversial, it managed to retain its 'alternative feel' (Munteanu 2017). However, in late 2018 Tumblr announced that from December 17 it would ban all 'adult content' from the service, leading many users to question the very purpose of the platform, because they had primarily turned to it as a safe space to explore controversial or taboo subjects.

Associated more with creating content, Tumblr will feature in my study in relation both to fan cultures and the sharing of creative writing, and with regard to author and reader interactions. Tumblr is also interesting for its facilitation of multimedia creative outputs, and for the formation of strong networks and communities. For example, Tumblr is responsible for launching innumerable Internet **memes**, and its mythology involves stories about users who have secured book deals based on their blogs. Though it is associated with community and with fun activities, Tumblr has proved highly controversial, attracting criticism for seemingly condoning plagiarism, pornography and posts promoting suicide and self-harm.

Instagram and Snapchat

While this study is concerned with the production of literary texts primarily in the form of writing, as I will argue in Chapters 1 and 3, contemporary literature is often **multimodal** and consumed across media. In addition, in keeping with social media's 'visual turn' and the emergence of distinctive 'platform vernaculars' (Gibbs et al. 2015), reader engagement with literary texts may be primarily visual, for example taking photos of books or capturing the reading moment on Instagram (discussed further in Chapter 4). For these reasons, the study will explore forms of literary production and engagement on Instagram and Snapchat.

Instagram, launched in 2010, is a social networking service primarily associated with the sharing of photographs or videos, allowing users to locate the images through the use of **geotags**, and to choose from various filters to modify and customise their images, as well as connecting their images to those of others through the use of hashtags. Instagram was bought by Facebook in 2012, and while Facebook's influence was minimal for many years, the growing popularity of the platform and the departure of the founders in 2018 fundamentally changed the dynamic between the parent company and one of its prime assets (Newton 2018).

Instagram has consistently added new features to its service, one of the most notable being its 'Stories' feature, which allows users to share 'all the moments of your day' in slideshow format, promises to relieve users from the fear of 'overposting', and reassures them that their posts will disappear after 24 hours. In late 2018, Instagram started testing 'creator accounts' with special features for influencers and creators with large followings, raising the possibility of a two-tier system for users based on their popularity that could prove to be highly controversial.

Instagram's Stories appears in many ways to be placing itself in direct competition with Snapchat, an app primarily associated with younger users distinguished by its philosophy that 'life's more fun when you live in the moment'. Users can share images and short videos that 'self-destruct' after 24 hours, adding lenses and filters and, as with Instagram, creating stories which link and tag images. Although the removal of images after 24 hours is its Unique Selling Point (USP), Snapchat reminds users that it is possible for others to store and record their images (for example by taking screenshots), and in 2016 it introduced a Memories feature to facilitate editing, searching and organising 'snaps' so that they can be saved. In early 2018 another redesign of the app prompted a petition topping over one million signatories who complained that the attempt to clearly separate celebrities and 'influencers' from 'friends' went against the whole ethos of Snapchat.

In his study of Snapchat, Lehner (2014) examines how it promotes and markets content mainly to 'millennials', and primarily with regards to broadcast media. For example, Lehner discusses how US television show *Girls* used Snapchat to update fans on news about the show, and how UK based soap opera *Hollyoaks* used Snapchat to reveal the identity of a murderer. However, his study points to the interesting ways in which the seeming limitations of its user base and the restrictions in terms of how it can be used, may in fact be the key to its growing success.

Meanwhile, Walker Rettberg (2018) charts Snapchat's development from an app mainly associated with the sharing of private messages to a media platform that can be used for disseminating news and commercial content. She argues that Snapchat is the antithesis of the world wide web as it is not about archiving or retrieving content so much as providing 'a constantly moving stream' (118) based on immediacy and intimacy and highly ritualised performances such as the 'good night photo'. Nevertheless, Walker Rettberg links the ephemerality of Snapchat to earlier media forms, notably television before the days of domestic recording equipment, and tries to explore how it has evolved to appeal to older users and to provide users with stories and some sense of continuity. She also argues that Snapchat has developed its own aesthetic, particularly through the use of lenses and filters that allow users to personalise content.

Madrigal (2018) argues that both Instagram and Snapchat, attracting mainly younger users, are less focused on virality than platforms like Facebook or Twitter where the demands of constant linking and retweeting can become repetitive and burdensome. Both Instagram and Snapchat have become associated with developments in augmented reality, allowing images or text to be overlaid on the 'real' world. Therefore, while they may be associated primarily with 'fun' and 'play' they have the potential to shape technological innovation and open up new ways of experiencing and creating fictional worlds. Academic studies of Instagram are few and far between, partly because of the restrictions on access (Caliandro and Gandini 2017). Existing studies have tended to focus on the presentation of the self and the phenomenon of the 'selfie' (Lim 2016; Warfield, Cambre and Abidin 2016). However, the growing field of Instagram studies is beginning to recognise the potential for the space to offer unprecedented access to the everyday rituals and private moments of social actors.

YouTube

Although YouTube appears in van Dijck's (2013) typology as a site primarily for hosting user-generated content, it includes a networking and 'social' aspect where users comment on each others' posts, or link or adapt content created by others. YouTube has emerged as a popular site for '**bookbloggers**' and 'vloggers' who review literary texts, as well as for creators of webseries based on classic literature, one of the most well-known being The Lizzie Bennet Diaries. The ways in which contemporary readers revisit, adapt, modernise and merge established literary works will be a major focus of this study, particularly in Chapter 2. Moreover, YouTube is a key site for the discussion of the emergence of the 'citizen critic' (Eberly 2000) as well as for promoting and publicising new literary works (discussed in Chapter 6).

Pinterest

Closely associated with the predominantly female activities of scrapbooking and collage, Pinterest can be distinguished from other forms of social media because of its focus on found content rather than user-generated content. According to Rodger's (2019) study of readers' use of Pinterest to catalogue, curate and promote their bookish behaviour, it is generally expected that content posted or 'pinned' by users is not owned or generated by them, and private pinning which does not allow for sharing and 'repinning' is actively discouraged. Moreover, drawing on the work of Postill and Pink (2012), Rodger argues that Pinterest is less about community than looser forms of 'digital sociality'. Rodger cites statistics showing more than 175 billion pins and 250 million monthly active users, and though she sees it as a space for users to work on projects and interests she acknowledges critiques (particularly Jones 2016) that examine how the labour of 'pinners' may be exploited and the extent to which Pinterest boards encourage a kind of self-surveillance for its mainly female users. While I have not found Pinterest to be a particularly significant platform particularly as regards literary expression or formations, I will return to Rodger's study of bookish displays on Pinterest in Chapter 4.

Inevitably, my discussion will be selective and reflective of the fact that the landscape or ecosystems I am trying to capture are constantly in flux, not only in terms of their terms and conditions and architecture, but also in terms of their ownership. Dominated by an oligopoly of powerful global corporations, notably Google and Facebook, many of the social media platforms discussed here began life as non-profit start-ups before being bought out by the oligopoly, often much to the disgust of users. While this study is not primarily concerned with the political economy of social media, ownership and management of the platforms will be a concern, as will the extent to which these large corporations exploit and monetise the creativity and emotional labour of users, so crucial to making the platforms work. While my main focus is on platforms that allow for the creation of content, rather than for example messaging apps, my discussion will try to reflect on changing usage and practice, as well as considering the impact of changes to both traditional and new media and how these influence the production and reception of cultural content, for example the emergence of on-demand services, second screening, binge watching and 'Netflixisation'.

Implications of social media for literature

This study is shaped by the belief that social media makes it easier than ever to look beyond literary texts to examine the infrastructures and relationships that shape their creation, dissemination and reception. While I am wary of technological determinism, I am interested in the ways in which the literary experience offered by social media varies from platform to platform, and challenges many of our prevailing assumptions about the 'social', memory and the idea of the self. In particular, notions such as that of the 'networked self' (Papacharissi 2013: 207) where 'self-identity in public and private life … traverses distinct yet connected planes of interaction or networks' have implications for both individuals and social contexts as they are represented *in* works of literature and for understanding the societies and individuals that produce, disseminate and respond to those same works.

Likewise, social media, in combination with the growing popularity of wearable technologies, has given rise to the notion of the 'quantified self' where one's sense of value and self-worth is measured and counted according to the number of followers or 'likes' one has, and where our actions and behaviours become trackable by others. Meanwhile, the concept of the 'spatial self' (Schwartz and Halegoua 2015) links self-presentation online to physical activity and location, allowing for a playful, game-like approach to self-expression while at the same time monitoring individuals based on where they are or where they are going. Finally, social networking sites facilitate complex, sometimes even contradictory ways of curating the self and constant rewards for authoring the story of the self (Paparachissi 2013) which may even extend into the afterlife as people's profiles and social media accounts continue to be active after they have died. Writers and poets have always wrestled with these complex negotiations of the self, the public and the private, the individual and society, but in the social media age they are embedded into our daily lives and routines in ways that present new opportunities as well as new anxieties.

In the chapters that follow, I will be returning to the question of how social media presents new challenges in terms of our experience of time. In particular, I will argue that social media's focus on **'nowness'** (Fiske 1987; Thomas 2014a), constant updating and quantification influences both the kinds of literature being created, and how that literature is consumed, shared and discussed. Likewise, the phenomenon of 'following' individuals, events or topics across time potentially offers new ways of observing things in process and getting closer to the dailiness of life. Social media also poses fundamental challenges to attempts to sustain distinctions between off- and online, between daily routine, entertainment and the life changing. In making open and accessible many of the processes, relationships and choices that go into making the literary possible, social media forces us to consider in new ways issues of **canonicity**, taste, quality, and how we value acts of reading, criticism and interpretation.

Chapter 2 will explore how literary writers have responded to and **remediated** new technologies, focusing particularly on humorous or satirical responses and attempts by authors to engage with social media and the affordances of specific platforms. However, I will also be considering darker visions, for example crime novels where the affordances of social media become the modus operandi of criminals and killers, or fictions that portray growing disillusionment and suspicion with the role of social media in our lives. In perhaps one of the most devastating and sustained representations of the impact of social media on our everyday lives, Dave Eggers' *The Circle* (2013) presciently conveys how the global corporations behind social media platforms inspire a cult-like following amongst devotees. Eggers' tale follows the story of Mae as she is initiated into the world of The Circle where to 'participate' becomes a chore and something that is scored and ranked mechanistically. However, Mae finds herself inexorably drawn back into the illusion of a 'world where everyone could know each other truly and wholly' (491) even if that means ultimately betraying those closest to her.

Methods

The digital humanities has emerged in many ways as a response to the proliferation of new literary and artistic cultures online and as a way of dealing with the vast quantities of information about readers, audiences and users that the digital makes visible, and I will be outlining some of the work representative of this shift in Chapter 4. However, while I recognise the usefulness and attractiveness of the methods that have emerged for capturing and (re)presenting this data, I am wary of the risk of abstraction that this focus on datafication (Livingstone 2018) can bring. I prefer instead to try to capture those discordant and resistant practices and responses that can so easily be muted or blurred where the emphasis is on generalising about emerging trends or commonalities between users.

My training as a literary critic means that my primary method for conducting research is textual analysis. However, it has also made me especially sensitive to issues of context, so whenever I encounter a new literary work on social media I want to understand the infrastructure of the platform, the practices that go on there, and the communities who share, discuss and circulate texts amongst each other. As my research has taken me beyond the text to consider not only these aspects of production and consumption contexts, but the individual responses of readers/audiences/users, I have turned to methods for audience research from media and cultural studies, as well as reception studies. Through my work on fanfiction and online communities, I have become familiar with methods such as **participant observation** and digital ethnography, and the ethical issues arising from what can be perceived as intrusion into the worlds and experiences of those communities (Thomas and Round 2016). A key starting point for my research on digital readers was the notion that the digital age makes available all sorts of found data and my practice is to work with evidence of participation rather than, for example, using questionnaires or interviews where I as the researcher set the parameters for the study. I have included material from one interview in Chapter 6 for information relating to emerging publishing practices, but in other chapters I base my findings on observation conducted in many cases over months and years.

Digital ethnography (Pink et al. 2016) and **netnography** (Kozinets 2010) are widely used terms which bring together cross-disciplinary approaches to methods and ethics for internet and social media research. Both draw from traditional ethnography and its focus on observing what users and participants are doing in a particular social context, while constantly reflecting on the role of the observer and the limitations of what can be observed. Discussion of methods from these perspectives has also led to the questioning of the key concept of community for online groupings (discussed further in Chapter 5), and their applicability to the kinds of 'me-centred formations' (Pink et al. 2016) characteristic of social media. For some the term 'networked individualism' (Pink et al. 2016) is more accurate for capturing the ways in which individuals connect with others and form distinctive nodes, without the utopian connotations and lack of specificity of 'community'. Another key feature of digital ethnography is its focus on the mediated nature of contact between individuals in online spaces, as well as the disruption of the dualistic division of on- vs offline behaviours and ways of being. Limitations of these methods include the potential for confirmation bias, while immersion in a particular community or prolonged engagement with key individuals can bring their own challenges in terms of maintaining objectivity (see Thomas and Round 2016).

Ethical issues affecting the study of online environments and social media have increasingly become an object of study in themselves. The Association of Internet Researchers has established an ethics working committee and published a set of recommendations in 2012 that are widely used and debated at the association's annual conference. In fan studies, the journal *Transformative Works and Cultures* regularly features articles on ethical and methodological matters including discussions of goodwill (Kelley 2016) and exploitation of fan labour (Jones 2014). In 2017, a special issue of *Applied Linguistics Review* on the ethics of online research methods considered the particular challenges posed for interdisciplinary research where competing ethical protocols may have to be negotiated, as well as the complex issues around ownership arising from social media data where the precise source of a piece of communication may be obscure. Scholars have also considered the implications of researching online in terms of feedback loops (Whiteman 2012; Thomas and Round 2016), where the subjects of research studies may feel entitled to speak out and answer back to the claims made about them. In my own practice, I have become more alert to the need to consider the sensitivities around reproducing online materials even where they are in the public domain (Thomas 2017), and to aim for transparency and reflexivity (Page 2017) where the balance between protecting subjects and providing depth and accuracy of analysis may be difficult to manage.

My approach to the critical analysis of content from social media may be defined as 'bottom up' in the sense widely used by narratologists and stylisticians (e.g. Bell, Ensslin and Rustad 2014) whereby discussion and analysis respond to current or emerging practice rather than attempting to provide a general typology or abstract theoretical overview. I also interpret the literary quite broadly, to include genre and popular works as well as reworkings and adaptations of existing texts.

One of the challenges of writing about new technologies is the rapid pace of change and the ephemerality not just of individual contributions but of the very platforms and technologies themselves. Over the last twenty or thirty years, we have arguably witnessed the accelerated obsolescence of new communication technologies, with constant upgrades to hardware and software and the rapid appearance and disappearance of devices and platforms. The emerging field of media archaeology attempts to help us recover the memory of what it was like to play space invaders as an arcade videogame or listen to music on a Sony Walkman. Yet many of the artefacts produced by earlier forms of technology are now impossible to access other than through the often unreliable accounts of users, or static screenshots. With studies of the rapidly changing landscape of social media, theorists are having to pay close attention to changes to terms and conditions and to the constant adding or removal of new features, so that at least we can begin to understand how usage changes, even if we cannot predict future changes or advances.

Policies concerning the reproduction of content posted on social media rightly protect individuals who may never have considered the implications of making that content freely available in the public domain.

However, in the context of conducting an academic study of literary outputs and discussions, some of these policies can be quite restrictive, particularly with regards to posts which feature images, videos or sound where ownership and copyright is hard to trace. In addition, accounts come and go, the management of accounts may change over time, and some accounts are entirely automated. In the discussions that follow, where possible permission has been sought from authors, commenters and posters whose words I reproduce from social media accounts. I also observe the specific terms and conditions of the platforms and apps I discuss and explicitly refer to these where relevant. Where content originally appearing on social media has been anthologised or reproduced in print form, I treat this in the same way as I would other published literary work.

Discussion of social media to date is largely confined to the Anglophone world. Given this, it is all too easy to overstate the take up of the digital globally, and of course there can be significant variations between regions and languages in terms of available platforms, digital literacy and so on. For example, the Electronic Literature Organization's database of electronic literature (discussed in Chapter 1) demonstrates how uneven engagement still is, at least in terms of works produced. While studies are emerging that focus on how social media is used by indigenous communities (Carlson and Frazer 2018) or that examine phenomena such as 'Black Twitter' (Florini 2013), the focus remains on political and social activism or countering marginalisation rather than on social media as a way of expressing or sharing creativity from within these communities.

In the chapters that follow I hope to provide readers with a window on some of the emerging literary practices that are particular to, though not necessarily uniquely found on, social media. I also hope to be able to offer insights and critical reflections on the implications of these emerging trends and practices for our understanding of the literary in the digital age. While I will acknowledge and discuss concerns about social media and the future of literature in the digital age, ultimately I remain optimistic regarding the possibilities for creativity, sharing and subversion that users exploit and display on a daily basis, and the potential this experimentation and play has for moving, stimulating and challenging others.

1 From the Holodeck to the Tweetdeck: electronic literature, interactivity and participation

As discussed in the Introduction, writers have always been fascinated by the emergence and impact of new technologies, and in the next chapter I will consider how this has sometimes involved attempting to recreate or remediate the affordances of new media and forms of communication within the existing parameters of traditional print-based literary genres. In this chapter I will explore how, from the 1980s onwards, writers and artists have created literary works that depend on computer technologies for their very existence, in order to better understand the specific ways in which literary outputs on social media have evolved both as a response to, and reaction against, some of those earlier experiments.

The 'End of Books'?

The increased affordability and usability of the 'home' computer in the 1980s led to the emergence of 'electronic' literature, defined by Rettberg (2018: 203) as writing created by or on computers which responds to the affordances of new technologies and is characterised by a 'sense of play and wonder'. In particular, a form of fiction utilising hyperlinks came to prominence, raising questions about the new possibilities for **interactive storytelling**, and leading to often apocalyptic predictions about the imminent 'End of Books' (Coover 1992). Most notably, in *The Gutenberg Elegies: The Fate of Reading in and Electronic Age*, Birkerts (1994) confronted the possibility of the displacement of the page by the screen to the detriment of 'the stable hierarchies of the printed page' (3) and asked whether the triumph of the digital meant the inevitable alteration of the '"feel" of literary engagement' (6). Although Birkerts does express optimism that 'literature [will] be able to prove the reports of its death exaggerated' (197), he can only conceive of this in terms of a need to seek out 'the word on the page' (197) and return to the book as a 'haven' from the digital. In the 1980s these fears about the end of books focused not so much on the threat posed by alternative delivery systems for literature (as would emerge later with the advent of ereaders), but on the changing roles of authors and readers, and on the ways in which interactive fiction in particular seemed to challenge the idea of the book as a stable, fixed object with clear beginnings, middles and ends, or recognisable characters, plots and settings.

Murray's *Hamlet on the Holodeck* (1997) offered one of the most enthusiastic responses to the new possibilities afforded by computer technologies, exploring continuities with existing literary traditions and celebrating the increased opportunities for participation that these technologies offered, as well as drawing links and parallels with games and other media texts (Murray's title alludes to an episode of the US tv show *Star Trek*). In response to these new possibilities, Murray and others developed a whole new cultural metalanguage (Manovich 2001) for talking about narrative structure and the role of the reader. Metaphors for narrative structure emerged based on the idea of the text as a maze, offering multiple pathways for the reader to navigate. Moreover, Murray's study relied heavily on the language of performance and simulation, highlighting how the computer facilitated the generation of new fantastical and immersive worlds that users could both play *in* and *with*. Murray and Birkerts became closely identified with the debates around digital literature and storytelling during this period, at one point in 1997 taking part in a head to head 'brain tennis' session at MIT. In 2017, *The New Yorker* published an article on Murray's book 'Twenty Years Later', highlighting how the book had foretold many of the innovations we now take for granted. But more importantly, perhaps, it argues that her book showed us that 'the digital moment must be understood as an extension of history, rather than a new beginning or a terrible end' and that 'digital space must be understood as deeply enmeshed in the existing cultural terrain' (Margini 2017).

Defining the field

To this day, discussion continues about how to define and what to call the field of study for emerging forms of literature which rely for their very existence on computer technologies or the digital. Rettberg (2018) recalls some of these debates in *Electronic Literature*, where he attempts to provide a typology of the main genres. He provides some interesting insights into what motivates writers to experiment with a new medium, suggesting that this is prompted by a need to explore 'How do I write in it?' while for readers the key question is 'How do I read it?' But he further argues that electronic literature is not just about playing with the possibilities of new media or interfaces, providing as it does interventions into debates about contemporary literature more broadly by defamiliarising its practices and providing the criticial distance necessary to understand and evaluate its contribution and value. For Rettberg, therefore, electronic literature's influences and antecedents are modernism and postmodernism, Dadaism and surrealism, not popular cultural or contemporary media and transmedia practices.

In his study, Rettberg considers whether we should talk of electronic literature in terms of projects rather than works, to convey that they may never reach a state of fixity or completion, as well as the fact that they may be accessed across different platforms or 'venues' (2018: 7). He further suggests that the concept of genre is especially useful in this context for establishing frames of reference for grouping together artefacts and practices as well as offering audiences a sense of 'how to read'. While Rettberg avoids referring to technology as a determining factor in terms of identifying the genres of electronic literature, he argues that an understanding of the 'capabilities and limitations of systems, platforms, and software' (11) are essential to their understanding. This is particularly true for the 'combinatory poetics' which Rettberg traces back to experimental writing traditions including Surrealist automatic writing and the works (or projects?) of the Oulipo (Ouvroir de littérature potentielle). In relation to social media, the influence of these movements is most obvious in computer-generated poetry and work which uses algorithms and **bots** for creative play (discussed in Chapters 2 and 3) as well as more broadly, as Rettberg recognises, in terms of focusing on the 'potential' of the literary as an ongoing and shared process.

Another key question raised by these new kinds of electronic literatures was precisely what the object of study would be. Thus concepts such as that of the page seemed to require redefining in the context of web pages that are dynamic and continually refreshed, while the idea of closure became problematic where texts had no clear or agreed sense of an ending. Lovell (2019: 80) has coined the term 'session-length promise' to refer to the ways in which content providers in the digital realm need to search for ways to signal to users how long they need to commit to a piece in any one session: in a traditional novel this is more straightforwardly a chapter, in games a level, and on tv an episode. One of the challenges for readers of digital and interactive fiction is that there often is no such sense of what constitutes a session, in addition to difficulties with starting again from where they left off and rereading (Thomas 2007b). For writers of electronic literature, meanwhile, the problems of defining the literary object or text manifest in pressing and practical issues related to intellectual property and monetising content.

The Brave New World of hypertext fiction

Ted Nelson's development of the concept of **hypertext** as a branching and responding text read on a computer screen (Barnet 2018) helped generate a whole new kind of labyrinthine writing often traced back to the literary experiments of Jorge Luis Borges. Indeed, like Borges's fictional 'Library of Babel', Nelson's earlier vision of Project Xanadu had sought to create a computer filing system capable of storing and delivering the great body of literature, and to make it possible for readers to annotate, link and compare documents with ease (Barnet 2018).

In addition to revolutionising writing, the emergence of hypertext fiction in the 1980s led to scrutiny of the act of reading. Not only was it impossible to fix on an agreed version of what a reading of any of these texts might look like, but the ways in which they were accessed might vary, for example whether on floppy disk or CD Rom, on a PC or a Mac. Reading or **'wreading'** thus came to be conceived as a potentially creative and liberatory practice, much as the term 'prosumer' has become commonplace in discussion of online spaces and social media. Whereas critics such as Landow (1992) celebrated the unique pleasures and satisfactions of these kinds of writing, nevertheless questions of coherence and quality recurred, perhaps because of the tendency of these 'first wave' (Bell, Ensslin and Rustad 2014) theorists to constantly compare the digital to print. Studies of these new forms of literature and the computer as a 'writing space' (Bolter 2001) furthermore tended to dwell on the 'problems' they pose for long held ideals of high culture as a unifying force, and for any shared concept of a literary canon.

Electronic literature has long had to contend with issues around discoverability. Unlike print books, whose covers and front and back matter can contain marketing materials in the form of endorsements or striking images, even in floppy disk or CD Rom formats, packaging for hypertext fictions was relatively uninspiring. Although some hypertext fictions have been anthologised in print and so have been marketed as books and can be found in bookshops, this is the exception rather than norm. Outside of the word of mouth within the academic and artistic communities, therefore, it can be difficult for anyone interested in exploring electronic literature to know where to start.

Nevertheless, texts from this period have been canonized (Ensslin 2007) and given validity by various cultural intermediaries. Many of the key producers of hypertext fiction – in particular Michael Joyce and Jane Yellowlees Douglas – were also among its most visible theorists and critics. Concerned more with formal innovation than engagement with readers, these writers positioned themselves very much in the experimental, avant-garde tradition.

For example, Michael Joyce often referred to himself playfully as the 'lesser Joyce', and his works share the modernists' predilection for the reworking of classical myths. Likewise, much 'first wave' criticism and theory drew heavily on structuralist and poststructuralist theory in attempting to think through the implications of these new forms.

A select group of hypertext writers enjoyed the security and patronage of Eastgate, an online publisher. Eastgate's Storyspace 'environment' was both developed and widely used by hypertext writers, but additionally acted as a kind of guarantor of quality, presenting itself as 'the primary source for *serious* hypertext' [my emphasis]. Eastgate was also an unashamedly commercial venture, ensuring that writers would benefit financially from their ventures by charging consumers for accessing content. Whether we see Eastgate as the catalyst of an emerging literary movement or as a barrier to access perhaps needs to be considered historically. Nevertheless, it is true to say that most of the high-profile proponents of hypertext fiction were academics or academic affiliated writers based in North America.

For some critics of hypertext fiction (e.g. Miller 1998; Mangen and van der Weel 2015), one of the main problems was that very few people actually wanted to read it. Despite the much vaunted claims of interactivity, little evidence has emerged of the creators of these fictions ever interacting with actual readers in any meaningful sense. Thus critics such as Hammond (2016: 155) seem to revel in the fact that hypertext fiction 'is one of the few digital literary forms that can be plausibly regarded as dead', and he claims its only true legacy is theoretical. Nevertheless, in addition to prompting increased debate about literary reading, literary texts, narratorial control and literariness itself, many hypertext fictions have become key texts in provoking discussion of the posthuman, embodiment and the complex forms of 'intermediation' between the medium of the body and other media (Hayles 2008). For example, Shelley Jackson's *Patchwork Girl* (1995), in which the reader navigates the narrative via the various body parts of the Frankensteinian central character, has been celebrated for the ways in which it 'explores the gendered body as the site of complex transactions and intermediation' (Goody 2011: 163). Moreover, hypertext fictions such as Jackson's help show how the new technologies of the computer and the internet require us to rethink concepts around identity and selfhood discussed in the Introduction, where the stability and reliability of memory is constantly being challenged, and where the idea of self as part of a network or system means that we are constantly reassessing our impressions of character and their interrelations.

Beyond hypertext and the impact of Web 2.0

In addition to an online publisher, electronic literature has its own journal, association and conference, as well as its own online collection aiming to help users locate the 'good stuff' (Hayles 2008: 40). Meanwhile 'New Media Writing' now has its own annual international prize (www. newmediawritingprize.co.uk), while 'interactive fiction' makes hypertext more user-friendly with open-source tools such as **Twine** (www.twinery. org) and Genarrator (www.genarrator.org) making it possible for writers to explore and play with nonlinear storytelling without having to grapple with (or pay for) the more established Storyspace. Nevertheless, some thirty years after the heyday of hypertext fiction, the search for an audience continues: in 2017 the writing competition Opening Up Digital Fiction (https://readingdigitalfiction.com/writing-competition/) set out to disseminate 'popular' and 'mainstream' interactive fiction to a 'broader segment of the public'.

Netprov or networked improvised literature provides a variant of electronic literature closely associated with social media because of its greater focus on collaboration and participation. As practised by Rob Wittig and Mark Marino, this kind of writing sets out to experiment with the ways in which 'social media can function as an environment and stage for new kinds of participatory performance' (Rettberg 2018: 175), as in the piece *Grace, Wit & Charm* (2012), which blends Twitter and live theatre, and *I Work for the Web* (2015), a satirical piece exposing 'the absurdities of common behaviours on social media' (Rettberg 2018: 178). Rettberg's account of Netprov links it with writing prompts and games, and he describes it as a structured form of collective writing. Nevertheless, while Netprov does allow for more active engagement from users than some other forms of electronic literature, it remains true that the artistic and creative conception of the piece is still very much under the control of the lead writers.

Often left out of discussions of electronic literature from this period, the work of Judy Malloy on social media practice dates back to 1986 and involves what Malloy calls an aleatoric process of slowly releasing fragments online, until the whole is completed. Malloy's *Uncle Roger* has been painstakingly preserved and reproduced in various formats, including Malloy's own 'Narrabase' (1991). Digital pioneers such as Malloy and Howard Rheingold (discussed further in Chapter 5) have provided fascinating insights into the emergence of distinctive communities of practice around new media writing and art, and corrective histories to the lazy description of emerging forms as new or unprecedented. For example, Rheingold's (2017) enthusiastic account of Netprov points to improvised storytelling on earlier platforms, such as Usenet and Compu-serve, and to collaborative projects such as *Invisible Seattle* (1983) which commissioned 'literary construction workers' to go out into the city to find contributors.

Nevertheless, electronic literature remains closely associated with nonlinear texts that foreground the activity and agency of the reader. Both the theory and practice of electronic literature also demonstrate a close connection with performance and gaming. For example, Ensslin's (2014) work situates itself on a 'literary-**ludic** spectrum', arguing both for the literariness of some videogames and for the game-like qualities of digital fictions. Although electronic literature is now about much more than words and text, a strong focus on language and formal experimentation persists.

Creators of hypertext fiction and early forms of electronic literature not only perceived themselves to be in the vanguard of experimentation with literary form, but also had to be technically proficient, under-standing code and software as well as the commercial imperatives affecting the distribution and uptake of their works. Novelistic repre-sentations of computers and communication technologies from the same period primarily portrayed them as mechanistic or alienating, a threat to culture and civilisation, or as the trigger for comic scenes based on the ineptitude of users (Thomas 2012). By the end of the twentieth century, however, there is undoubtedly a growing sense of inevitability about the role of technology in the production and consumption of literary texts, with computers becoming less of a curiosity and more of a necessity for writers. Interviewed in 2000, Martin Amis admitted to relying more and more on his computer, despite describing this shift as 'sinister', and bemoaning the loss of the 'slightly painterly feel' of writing in longhand (Richards 2000). At the beginning of the twenty-first century and with the arrival of **Web 2.0**, technology became much more user friendly, facilitating greater openness and access both in terms of the consumption and production of cultural content online.

Whereas in the 1980s when hypertext fiction was at its peak, computers would mainly have been accessed in the workplace, as the technology advanced and devices for accessing the internet became more portable, the technology and associated practices become much more embedded in people's daily routines.

Web 2.0 brought more opportunities for users to customise and per-sonalise content, making the choices that seemed so revolutionary in hypertext fiction look positively restricted and simplistic. As Barry (2018: 68) puts it, with Web 2.0 the net exists 'less to provide static pages for users to consume, and more to allow those users to actively intervene in adding music, video, opinion, and information of their own'. This had implications, too, for the literary, since as Hammond (2016: 175) notes 'As the computer has transitioned from a device capable of transmitting only numbers and text to one able to carry multiple modalities, it has increasingly brought into question the notion of "literariness"'. However, it is important to remember once again that this shift is not solely determined by technological change, but is equally the result of the profound cultural shifts observed by Collins (2010) and others as literature adapts to rather than competes against other media and cultural forms. Moreover, these cultural shifts did not take place in isolation from wider social and political changes and commercial imperatives. In 1995 online retailer Amazon set out to treat books as shiftable 'content' and undercut traditional gatekeepers with its innovative but controversial retail and distribution strategies. As will be discussed further in Chapter 4, digitisation has affected not only the way in which literary texts are produced and marketed, but also how they are accessed and studied, making it possible to summon up ancient manuscripts on screen, or engage in ever more sophisticated kinds of **distant reading**.

Readers/audiences/users

As was discussed earlier, many of the key innovations of hypertext fiction prompted searching questions about how readers accessed, engaged with and interpreted texts. Debates and anxieties about reading have, if anything, become more common with the advent of Web 2.0 and emerging practices such as 'migratory' reading (Parody 2011) where texts may be accessed across different devices and platforms, as well as ongoing concerns about dwindling attention spans. Hayles (2007) considers whether a distinction between 'hyper' and 'deep' attention reflects a generational divide in the way people think and process information in the digital age. However, she challenges any simplistic notion that one is 'better' than the other, as well as the idea that they can be easily plotted against the emergence of new technologies. In fact, she argues that the ability to focus deeply on something is a luxury for members of developed societies, with the ability to manage multiple information streams and to multi task having its own very tangible benefits in pressured situations. Thus multi- or transliteracy may be valuable skills for the 'attention economy' as we move from the mainly text-based experiments of hypertext authors onwards, and as digital literature has increasingly relied on multimodal effects.

Flores (2018) has proposed that, dating from 2005, we are witnessing the emergence of a 'third generation' of electronic literature, signalling mainstream adoption of emerging forms. He argues that elit creators now turn to existing platforms and mobile devices rather than building interfaces of their own, making it easier for readers/users to adapt skills they already have, for example swiping or rotating a screen on a smartphone. For the elit creator, according to Flores, this brings a ready-made mass audience, something that second and first wave artists could only dream of. However, he still draws a qualitative distinction between what he terms original and derivative works. Moreover, he conflates user-generated content that may not necessarily position itself as 'literature' with works by artists who had established themselves during what he describes as the 'modernist' second wave, suggesting that the relationship of elit to the mainstream is still far from unproblematic.

Another leading figure in the Electronic Literature Organization (ELO), Serge Bouchardon (2018), offered his reflections on what he calls the '10 gaps for Digital Literature', in an attempt to define what, if anything, makes digital (born) literature distinct from print-based varieties. Bouchardon admits to being wary of experiments on social media because of their dependence on proprietary platforms. However, in attempting to embrace emerging forms and practices, he calls for the study of digital literature to engage not just with words but gestures and animations. He reflects on the nomadic activity now required of readers and the ways in which neither the identity of the text nor its readers has a single trajectory, but multiple trajectories across different platforms. Another distinctive characteristic of digital literature, according to Bouchardon, is its ability to incorporate and be responsive to the reader's reality, both spatial and temporal, using data from the reader's 'real' world to drive and shape the work of fiction, particularly with regards to **locative** works, and those hosted on social media. Chapter 3 will provide analysis of some examples of fiction created for Twitter which rely on this kind of liminality and ontological uncertainty.

Fans, participatory cultures and transmedia storytelling

One of the key features of Web 2.0 was the increasing blurring of the boundaries between content producers and consumers, between professional writers and artists and those who might previously have been seen as amateurs or DIY enthusiasts. Perhaps this is most evident with regard to fanfiction, which has grown from a subculture of devotees creating and sharing stories based on beloved characters, plotlines and tropes from literature, tv and film in the form of limited runs of print zines, to the vast fan sites and communities now readily found online. Fanfiction raises questions about authorship and originality which will be taken up in more detail in the next two chapters. In addition, it has presented critics and theorists with new quandaries, both challenging existing notions of value and taste in relation to literature and posing new questions about the extent to which the lasting contribution or worth of a text can be considered in purely formal or aesthetic terms removed from the contexts in which that text is accessed and circulated (Thomas 2011b).

Crucial to Web 2.0, too, is the idea of community, and attempts to democratise the management and gatekeeping of content (see Chapter 5 for critiques of this notion). As was mentioned in the introduction, fan cultures are often associated with the idea of a gift economy and with reciprocal practices in terms of sharing content or providing feedback and support. Although undoubtedly hierarchies persist (Thomas and Round 2016), the roles of moderators and administrators on online discussion groups and fan forums are often shared and rotated, and the agreed terms and conditions or community guidelines are made available to users. Moderators and site admins are usually active participants in the communities they manage, and are highly committed to maintaining those communities and protecting them from outsiders (Thomas and Round 2016).

As outlined in the Introduction, Henry Jenkins has emerged as a key figure for mapping and understanding some of the conceptual and practical consequences of Web 2.0, particularly the notion of convergence between media, and the focus on participatory cultures centring on but not confined to the web. Jenkins has collaborated with literary scholars to show how the participatory ethos can be extended to encourage greater engagement with classic literature (Jenkins and Kelley 2013). His concept of participatory culture, emerging from his work on fandoms and fan cultures, is built on the premise that technology need not be seen as a barrier to participation, and that participation may in fact take many different forms: 'many will only dabble, some will dig deeper' (7). The concept of a participatory culture is also invested in the notion that desire for artistic expression is not confined to a select few, and that creative communities can be mutually supportive and collaborative.

Jenkins' influence can be seen not only in bringing into the discussion forms of creative expression previously marginalised but in shifting the focus in the study and theorising of electronic/digital/new media writing towards increased consideration of and engagement with users/readers/audiences (e.g. Page and Thomas 2011; Bell, Ensslin and Rustad 2014). Moreover, Jenkins' concept of transmedia storytelling has been influential in accounting for creative practice and design which specifically sets out to engage users across different media. As Jenkins defines this process, transmedia storytelling is 'a process where integral elements of a fiction get dispersed systematically across multiple delivery channels for the purpose of creating a unified and coordinated entertainment experience' (2007). Though Jenkins has often revised and refined the theory, and responded to its misuse by others, it helps to account not only for the activity of content producers and distributors, but also users, who have become accustomed to seeking out content across media, in Jenkins' parlance as modern day hunters and gatherers.

Literature on the go

With mobile computing comes the ability to consume content 'on the go', giving rise to specific media and literary forms designed to help pass time while on a commute. In Japan the 'keitai shosetsu' (cellphone novel) was a popular phenomenon in the early noughties, written by amateur authors (mainly young women) and distributed via websites such as Maho i-land to mainly young women (Goodyear 2008; see also Chapter 3). As well as making it possible for users to access content untethered, mobile devices connect to geo-spatial technologies (GPS/GIS), making it possible to create site-specific, location-based and location-aware works connecting users to their environment and creating new possibilities for writers to draw on urban and rural land and soundscapes in new ways. Locative works have additionally prompted a resurgence of interest in the idea of a spatial poetics, probing the liminal spaces between readers and characters/actors, and between fictional and real places.

Network aesthetics and the politics of new media

Early studies of electronic literature emerged primarily from the fields of narratology and literary linguistics. As with the advent of postclassical narratology (Page and Thomas 2011) and its response to the digital, contemporary studies of electronic literature look beyond formalist analysis, engaging more with the cultural politics and theoretical turns that have arisen in response to new forms and practices. For example, the fields of **Posthumanism** and **New Materialism** have provided critical reflection on and interrogation of concepts such as agency, ontology and relationality. In addition, they have been instrumental in moving debates about the digital beyond the kinds of essentialism and dualism so often in evidence especially in discussions about online vs offline worlds.

The rise of social networking sites has prompted discussion of the idea of a distinctive kind of network aesthetics (Jagoda 2016) exploring the relationship between cultural forms that network technologies make possible, while recognising how those forms and those networks are embedded in the fabric and routines of everyday life. Jagoda argues for a participatory aesthetics influenced in particular by video games, as well as new kinds of relational thinking. Likewise, Walker's (2004) work on blogs and early forms of social networking gave rise to her theory of **distributed narratives** which cannot be linked to a single author, a single place or moment, and which 'cross over into our daily lives' (discussed further in Chapter 3). Rettberg (2018) includes Network Writing as one of the main genres of electronic literature, arguing that this kind of writing can only take place once we have the internet, as writers respond to the nature of the network discourses that emerge to create works that are multimodal, distributed and scattered.

Another key development has seen the field of new media studies open up to engage more overtly with cultural politics and critiques of neoliberalism. For example, Kember and Zylinska in *Life After New Media* (2012) have argued for the need for the field to move beyond initial fascination with the new and a preoccupation with what makes new media different from that which went before. They argue that contemporary new media studies needs instead to look beyond the computer and find a way of bridging the humanities, with its focus on what media mean, and the social scientific concern with political and social influences and effects. Similarly, Chun (2016) critiques the whole idea of the 'new' in new media studies to consider the importance of the habitual and the kinds of effects and responses that may emerge after the first encounter. Chun also focuses on the importance of the concept of updating in digital cultures, arguing that we 'live and die by the update', while Thomas (2011a) has demonstrated how the expectation of constant updates results in a kind of processual aesthetic with authors and readers engaging in dialogue to shape and negotiate both the new media artefact or text and their mutual relations.

Critical accounts and studies of modernism and postmodernism have amply demonstrated the dangers of attempting to create a linear narrative of the evolution of literary movements, particularly where those may involve characterisation of audience largely built on generalisation or conjecture (discussed further in Chapter 5). Thus while it may be tempting to characterise electronic literature as occupying a similar kind of literary high ground as modernism, and to see participatory practices as engaging with popular culture and ontological boundaries in ways often associated with the postmodern, this would be to ignore the extent to which there is ongoing dialogue and mutual influence. Rather, the contemporary new media literary landscape is one where it may be more accurate to speak of co-existence and adaptation, but with a joint focus on continuing to challenge the boundaries of the literary and to explore the challenges posed by new technologies in terms of how they unsettle and shift out fundamental concepts and beliefs about ourselves and our world. The next chapter will examine how retellings and reimaginings of the literary, often neglected in the desire to focus on the 'new', may contribute to this complex process of adaptation and dialogue with tradition and the past.

2 Old wine in new bottles? Retelling and reimagining the literary with social media

The previous chapter dealt primarily with self-consciously experimental literature produced in response to emerging technologies. This chapter focuses on a different kind of response, in which artists, writers and everyday users play with existing literary outputs and forms, adapting them to new platforms and delivery systems, and demonstrating their continued significance for the contemporary context. Postmodern theory and increasing convergence between media have brought into sharp focus how contemporary 'cultural landscapes [are] flooded with remixes, remakes and reboots' (Parody 2011: 1). Likewise, the popularity and increasing influence of fanfiction demonstrates an appetite amongst ordinary readers and audiences to contribute to this process and to extend their engagement with the fictional worlds they feel so intimately connected to. One response to this would be to see it as symptomatic of a literature of exhaustion (Barth 1984 [1967]) faced with 'the used-upness of certain forms or the felt exhaustion of certain possibilities' (64). However, instead of despairing of 'the art that not many people can *do*' (65) perhaps a more positive take is to see these new 'intermedia arts' as posing important questions about originality and imitation, irony and intention.

Indeed, the Electronic Literature Organization Collection, discussed in the previous chapter, has a special section for remixes described as 'reworking of materials from one or several works to produce a new artistic creation' (http://collection.eliterature.org/3/keyword.html), though in this case the reworking is mainly of works by other ELO artists. In addition, the term 'Netprov', closely associated with the ELO (discussed in Chapter 1), places a strong emphasis on the creative use (or reuse) of available media (http://meanwhilenetprov.com). Netprov provides a good link between the more avant-garde experimentation of the artists involved in ELO remixes, and the kinds of grassroots creative projects enabled by Web 2.0 where users readily create their own remixes and 'mash ups' of cultural texts. As we shall see, these practices and their potential for subversion as well as creative play now pervade social media platforms, and open up seemingly limitless possibilities for interactivity, hybridity and liminality.

This chapter will begin by considering how social media has breathed new life into traditional literary forms and brought classic works to new audiences. Ever since the internet made it possible for users to create profiles for fictional characters or deceased luminaries, online spaces have provided an outlet for individuals and groups to share their passions, responses and creative reimaginings of literary authors and their works. My first introduction to this phenomenon was discovering an account for Jane Austen on the social networking site Myspace in the days when social networks almost exclusively focused on music. The profile for Jane Austen listed her hobbies, marital status and so on as for any other user, with the exception that her age was recorded as being over 200. Likewise, on Twitter one of the first accounts which captured my imagination was @DrSamuelJohnson, an account with tens of thousands of followers which purports to record the views of the 'gouty lexicographer' on current affairs. A similar idea underlines @LeVostreGC (or Chaucer Doth Tweet) commenting on news and popular cultural events in Middle English. These accounts reflect the widespread popularity of spoof and parody accounts across social media, particularly those focusing on celebrities. They may also be seen as contiguous with fan practices, and the appetite amongst fans for creatively engaging with the objects of their devotion through posting fan vids, fan art and fanfiction, often extending to and including the lives and personalities of the authors, particularly those behind expansive fictional universes. Pugh (2005) has argued that fans want both 'more of' and 'more from' the fictional universes they constantly revisit, meaning that both the vast potential of that universe, and their own ability to create within its confines, know no bounds.

Social media accounts based on literary works and authors

Retellings and reworkings of literary worlds take many forms and perform a variety of functions. Often the intent is primarily playful, as in the case of @limeritrature which boldly claims to offer followers 'A limerick version of every work of literature ever written' via Twitter. Marking anniversaries of literary figures' births and deaths is commonplace (discussed further in Chapter 6), as is the recording of landmarks with specific literary works and their publication. Furthermore, social media can be used for sharing letters, diaries and the lesser known works of well-known writers. Since 2008 @samuelpepys has been reproducing Pepys' historical diary entries 'in real time', introducing new audiences to the events of the period as though they are breaking news. So while some of the accounts feature original content that alludes to or is loosely based on existing forms, genres or works, in other instances the accounts actually reproduce content from historical and literary texts. As a number of these accounts have been in existence for some time, presumably they do not breach copyright as short tweets would come under 'fair use'.

Also on Twitter, @MsJeanRhys provides daily musings from the author drawing on a variety of sources including her novels, an unfinished autobiography, interviews and letters. Occasionally, an 'EDITOR' will intervene to identify the source or to engage in a caustic aside: 'If you respond to one of Ms Rhys's tweets, please be aware she is very, very unlikely to reply. Because she's dead' (18 July 2015). Followers of the account can not only expect daily tweets illuminating both the author's work and her life, but furthermore that the tweets are carefully chosen to reflect a date in the calendar (e.g. Valentine's Day), or to provide an ironic commentary on current affairs. For example, on 28 February 2018, dubbed 'snowmageddon' in the UK, @Ms Jean Rhys tweeted: 'I've thought about death a great deal. One day in the snow I felt so tired. I thought, Damn it, I'll sit down. I can't go on. I'm tired of living here in the snow and ice. So I sat down on the ground. But it was cold so I got up'. Many of the tweets refer to excessive consumption of alcohol and to an overpowering sense of melancholia or helplessness, though it is not always possible to tell at a glance if they are taken from the fictional works, or from the diaries and letters. While presumably both the author of the account and many of its thousands of followers are familiar with Jean Rhys and her works, the tweets resonate just as much because of their aphoristic commentary and world weary reflections on fairly mundane activities or events: 'I'll get up when I wish to. I'm very lazy you know' (8 February 2018).

Writers who excel in the aphoristic of course lend themselves well to Twitter. @DailyPlum (with over 7.5k followers as of November 2019) lives less and less up to its faint promise to provide a 'daily (more or less) dose of P.G. Wodehouse', but when it does, it provides followers with memorable lines from the comic master, particularly celebrating Wodehouse's fondness for extreme similes 'like a halibut that's taken offense [sic] at a rude remark from another halibut' (1 February 2018) and reproducing scenes of dialogue between some of the most loved comic pairings. Each of these tweets attracts a high number of retweets and likes, suggesting that for followers of this account there is great pleasure to be derived from Wodehouse's skill with language and speech. @Daily-Plum is one of a number of accounts devoted to Wodehouse and his comic creations, including @DailyWodehouse and @WodehousianWord, who continues the medical theme promising that 'Wodehouse words each day keeps the doctor away'.

Literary social media accounts are often the work of devotees keen to raise the profiles of neglected authors or works, or simply to share their passions. In many cases, the people behind the accounts are academics or members of learned societies devoted to an author or work. Wesley Raabe managed the @Mother Whitman account for around two years on Twitter, based on his work editing her letters for the Walt Whitman Archive. In an email to the list-serv for the Society for the History of Authorship, Reading and Publishing (SHARP), Professor Raabe (2018) reveals how his fondness for 'Twitter by dead people' was not enough to sustain him, citing lack of feedback as one of the main reasons why he gave up on the account. He recommends to others that they consider turning such accounts into bots that will automatically generate content so that the editor can 'untether yourself' from what can be a significant commitment.

Perhaps one of the more effective examples of the use of a bot for retelling a work of literature comes from @UlyssesReader which algorithmically 'reads' Joyce's novel 'slowly' for a following of over ten thousand. As well as presumably appealing to Joyce refuseniks by breaking up the notoriously difficult works into more easily digestible parcels (@Finnegansreader is a 'sister' project run on the same principle), the retelling allows devotees of Joyce to experience the texts anew. In addition to foregrounding the linguistic play and poetry of Joyce's writing, by bringing the text into the user's timeline, it creates a sense of immediacy and of a blending of the characters and their utterances into the routines and rhythms of the everyday (Thomas 2016). Other Joycean ventures on Twitter include @Ulyssesinaday, setting out to 'read' the novel via Twitter on 16 June 2015 following in the tradition of 'Bloomsday', but also 'Because no book is unreadable'. Alongside Joyce, Samuel Beckett also features on Twitter, which, according to Tranter (2016), should come as no surprise given that 'his compact observations and incisive remarks are perfectly trimmed for our social media age'. Tranter is behind the @samuelbbeckett account which he maintains to 'offer a glimpse of Beckett's unique tragicomic tone' in the hope that 'if I have prompted anyone to pick up one of his books or a ticket at the box office, I will know that I have failed better'.

Like Tranter and Raabe, Mark Semple, the man behind @MobyDickat-Sea based on Melville's novel, and @JustToSayBot generating variations on William Carlos Williams' poems, is an academic, in Semple's case with a particular interest in software studies and algorithmic culture. While these accounts demonstrate a playful attitude to the literary classic, they also raise serious and profound questions about the nature of authorship and originality where automated accounts can, judging by their popularity and the responses of followers, result in a more rewarding response to a literary text than in its original form. As with the Jean Rhys account, and as I will discuss more fully in Chapter 3, the impact of the individual tweets produced by these bots can only be understood in the context of the followers' timelines, and the coincidence or serendipity of their appearing at a particular time or at a particular place alongside tweets about all sorts of other events from the past and the present. But what clearly resonates with users is the ability of these literary tweets to capture a particular mood or moment even if reproduced out of any kind of context in terms of a 'text' or an author's work.

I will return in the next chapter to the question of how Twitter accounts and experiments with automation play with time and liminality. However, while bots may disrupt and play with notions of sequence and continuity in relation to existing literary works and how they are to be read, other retellings of classic works draw on strategies and devices for marking time and retaining the attention of audiences from traditional oral storytelling. As I have previously discussed (Thomas 2014a; Thomas 2016), Chindu Sreedharan's @epicretold, a retelling of stories from the Mahabarata from Bhima's point of view, set out to provide a serial narrative on an epic scale for followers to enjoy over a period of several years. @epicretold has acknowledged its debt to an already existing retelling of the Mahabarata in the form of a blog by Prem Panicker, itself based on a novel by M.T. Vasudevan (Sreedharan 2014), and the author explicitly reflects on his attempts both to react to the affordances of Twitter as a relatively new platform, as well as to master the art of 'protracted storytelling' (5). @epicretold therefore provides an interesting counterpoint to the idea that Twitterfiction is all about small stories (discussed further in Chapter 3), while also demonstrating that the form can be used to celebrate and reimagine 'classics' from beyond the Western literary canon.

New forms of participation

Although the accounts discussed so far are managed by individuals and are often specific to particular texts or authors, social media also provides opportunities for collaborative and participatory activities. This includes emoji retellings of classic novels including *Moby Dick* and *The Grapes of Wrath* (Flood 2016) and various kinds of hashtag games with a literary flavour, for example #replacebooktitleswithbacon in 2011 which generated entries including We Need To Talk about Kevin Bacon and The Hitchhiker's Guide to Bacon.

#folklorethursday is a weekly event taking place on Twitter where users post links or summaries of folk tales and customs from around the world using the shared hashtag. Activity is moderated by a central account

(@FolkloreThurs) which retweets content, comments on posts and thanks contributors. Occasionally, the account managers intervene to address abusive posts, although the hashtag is free for anyone to use, and many of those using the hashtag do so regularly and are clearly invested in sharing and preserving folk customs and tales, resulting in a strong sense of community. The fact that the activity is regularly scheduled contributes greatly to this sense of community, and follows a pattern established for users in other contexts on Twitter (e.g. #dorsethour, #yagym (The Welsh Hour)) where a particular hashtag and the community associated with it appear to take ownership of a small chunk of time.

Thus, in addition to the desire to improve or educate followers, literary accounts on social media offer users the opportunity to participate, whether that is by commenting, retweeting or simply liking posts. As will be discussed more fully in Chapter 6, social media provide a space for readers to share not only their reflections and responses with others, but the act of reading itself, whether that is by posting a photograph of the book they are reading, where they are reading it (as in bookstagramming discussed in Chapter 4), or by joining in with a group read, using hashtags to connect with others reading the same text. The performative capabilities of sharing classical literature via Twitter is further evident in 'live' shared readings of texts e.g. @GEReadalong (Reading ((and tweeting)) Dickens's *Great Expectations* as it first appeared in weekly instalments), and @Such_Tweet, an adaptation of Shakespeare's *Romeo and Juliet* improvised by actors from the Royal Shakespeare Company (RSC) across platforms including Twitter and YouTube for a limited period of time in 2010.

The target audience for these more participatory reworkings of classic literary texts is clearly the generation (X, Y, or Z) that has grown up with these platforms and a culture where the user expects to have to forage for more content, to follow links across platforms, and even to contribute content him or herself (Jenkins 2009). The Emmy award winning The Lizzie Bennet Diaries, based on Austen's *Pride and Prejudice*, had its own channel on YouTube and followed the plot of Austen's novel in the form of character vlogs. However, the format also encompassed interactive elements, such as Q&As with the audience. Such was the success of the series that several spin offs and imitators have followed, including Emma Approved, and Frankenstein M.D., produced by the makers of The Lizzie Bennet Diaries, and The Autobiography of Jane Eyre and Socially Awkward Edgar Allan Poe. Following on from the success of their social media experiment @Such_Tweet, the RSC has used Snapchat to invite users to 'become' *The Tempest*'s Ariel using an interactive lens, demonstrating once again how literary texts particularly invite these immersive responses as users relish the opportunity to enter the fictional worlds they have read about, or seen acted out, or performed in themselves.

In addition, many of these accounts clearly set out to appeal to students of classic literature seeking new ways to engage with the texts prescribed to them. In August 2018 the New York Public Library (@nypl) launched its InstaNovel series on Instagram with a digitized version of *Alice's Adventures in Wonderland* to be followed by an animated version of Charlotte Perkins Gilman's *The Yellow Wallpaper* and Kafka's *Metamorphosis*. Intended to provide new ways of accessing 'classics', the choice of initial texts (some of which may not be categorised as novels) is clearly focused on mobility ('perfect length for the subway commute', Brown 2018) but also visuality.

On Spark Notes, an online resource aimed at making classic works accessible, one of the writers created Snapchats from Classic Literature in May 2018 while the site's blog also has a feature on the dating app Tinder ('If Fictional Characters had Tinder'). Meanwhile Thug Notes on YouTube parodies the likes of SparkNotes, with 'gangster' language and colourful graphics providing irreverent insights into 'classic literature' including *One Flew Over the Cuckoo's Nest, No Country for Old Men* and *Animal Farm*. User engagement includes comments from subscribers suggesting what to cover next, as well as discussion of topics raised, such as whether the book or the film adaptation is superior. Each video refers the viewer to the website where the book *Thug Notes: A Street Smart Guide to Classic Literature* and other merchandise can be purchased.

Forms of engagement and participation with the classics on social media therefore bridges both commercial enterprises and community-based or fannish activity, with the boundaries between the two often becoming blurred. On platforms such as Tumblr and Instagram, users can create dedicated spaces for exploring and communicating their literary passions and express and share their passions visually (discussed further in Chapters 4 and 6). Sometimes tributes to authors and their works on these platforms extend to handicrafts (knitted dolls of Darcy and Elizabeth), foodstuffs (Harry Potter themed cookies) and body art (Twilight tattoos) which in many cases can be commissioned and purchased by other users. But the activities also have a strong community element, so the sharing of the artefact online is important, as is responding to the comments, suggestions and encouragement of others.

Generating faux classics, traditions and myths

The idea of 'spreadable media' (Jenkins 2013) and the phenomenon of virality associated with online cultures, means that such is the pace and scope of the dissemination, uptake and customisation of content across multiple platforms and from multiple sources that the whole idea of identifying and agreeing on a source or origin text can be contentious. Social media is fertile ground for the spreading of rumour and myth, and this has contributed to the emergence of genres such as '**creepypasta**', defined by Ondrak (2018: 162) as 'unsettling paranormal and horror content copied, pasted and remixed on social media and Web 2.0 platforms under the guise of real and lived encounters'. Referred to by some as a meme but by others as a unique kind of digital fiction (Ondrak 2018), sharing and customising content is intrinsic to creepypasta. Ondrak argues that the horror genre has always been highly adaptable to new advances in media and technology, as can be seen in some of the examples of Twitterfiction discussed in the next chapter. However, creepypasta can be seen as representing a new genre because of the fact it is so attuned to the affordances of the social media platforms (YouTube; Reddit; Twitter) on which it is primarily found. Indeed, Ondrak goes on to suggest that creepypasta can be seen as an example of **post-postmodern** storytelling in terms of its metatextuality and ongoing dialogue with postmodern horror narratives.

One of the websites dedicated to the phenomenon (www.creepypasta. com) provides an archive of what it calls the 'main' original pastas, but also invites new submissions and provides a forum for discussion. Slender Man is the most notorious example of the genre to date – a tall faceless man who makes children disappear, and who is said to have been an influencing factor driving two young girls to stab their friend. A documentary based on the story was produced by HBO in 2016, and the viral phenomenon has even produced academic studies (Chess and Newsom 2015) and its own subgenre of erotic fiction.

In his discussion of creepypasta, Ondrak (2018) notes that much of the attention given to the narratives so far focus on how they remediate folkloric storytelling styles and word-of-mouth communication associated with urban myths. He further traces the lineage of this kind of writing back to earlier tales of hauntings and ghostly encounters that exist in the '"in between" space' between 'the words on the page and the readers' minds' (163) and argues that crucial to understanding this new genre is the relationship between creators and readers, and the role the latter may play in improvising and extending the narrative.

Locating itself in a much longer tradition of the 'urban weird', @Hooklandguide has been sharing tales of 'Strange England' with its followers since 2014. I will be discussing how the account's author interacts with followers and shares and curates content from multiple sources in Chapter 6. But the account explicitly links itself with folklore and folk horror through hashtags featured on the account profile, as well as with literary critical movements such as **hauntology** and **psychogeography** which challenge and transgress temporal, historical and ontological boundaries, and which concern themselves with traces, the liminal and the not-quite-there.

Like the creepypasta phenomenon, and distributed narratives of the kind discussed in Chapters 1 and 3, the impact of these eerie posts relies in no small part on the blurring of the boundaries between fact and fiction. In particular, Hookland often draws on rumour, as in Figure 2.1 ('some say'), as well as snippets of folk wisdom (known as Hookland aphorisms). In addition, posts use black and white images of fictional landscapes (Barrowcross) and evocative locations to add to the sense of mystery and foreboding. For artists and writers keen to experiment with literary forms where the reader is an active participant in the creation of meaning, and where furthermore the reader's own temporal and material reality can potentially shape and influence the emerging story, this return to myth and legend in fact provides exciting new territory for play and exploration.

Hookland
@HooklandGuide

Following ∨

In the shadows cast by what remains of the Iron Age villages on Barrowcross, some say you can still smell wood smoke, hear laughter and shouts.

2:56 AM - 4 Dec 2018

Figure 2.1 Hookland's Barrowcross

New wine in old bottles: incorporating new technology in the novel

The advent and uptake of new computer technologies has not only prompted experimentation with these technologies and their affordances but also responses which remain resolutely within the domain of 'old' media. Bolter and Grusin (2000) refer to this process as **remediation**, whereby not only do new technologies constantly refer back to and refashion 'old' media, but 'old' media also attempt to assert their status and continued relevance by assimilating and refashioning aspects of the 'new'. Bolter and Grusin therefore both set out to challenge the myth of the new, and to show how emerging technologies look back to and pay homage to established, older forms and media. Thus, for example, they argue that the MUD (multi-user dungeon/domain) remediates the print novel (later qualifying this as a fantasy or romance novel). They also argue that *USA Today* visually resembles a multimedia computer application and that the CNN website borrows its sense of immediacy from televised newscasts. Rather than offer linear narrative accounts of the inexorable progress of technology, instead Bolter and Grusin focus on 'the ambivalent and contradictory ways in which new digital media function for our culture today' (2000:4).

Literature has a long history of authors responding to and borrowing from emerging media and communication technologies, but crucial to the idea of remediation, as Rettberg (2018) points out, is media reflexivity. So while some literary texts incorporate new technologies for the purposes of plot, they may feature to highlight and exacerbate struggles for communication between characters for comic purposes, as was the case with the telephone and telegram in the early twentieth century (Thomas 2012). Radio and film also feature in fiction from this period, and influenced the narrative techniques of both high Modernist writers such as Woolf and Joyce, and writers of comic fiction such as P.G. Wodehouse and Evelyn Waugh (Thomas 2012). The response to emerging technologies may therefore be wry as much as it is anxious, and even where there is suspicion or distrust, a fascination with the mechanics of new technologies and their implications for interaction and communication may be evident.

Novelists have also reacted to more recent technologies with humour: in David Lodge's *Small World* (1984) Professor Robin Dempsey is led by his special interest in linguistics, but also by his loneliness after the break-up of his marriage, to take part in an experiment involving ELIZA, a program designed "to enable computers to talk' (154) based on simulating psychiatrist–patient interviews and named after the character from Shaw's *Pygmalion*. While the novel gradually reveals that the experiment is a fake, and Dempsey its dupe, the exchanges between Dempsey and ELIZA are remarkably prescient about the dangers of relying too much on the kinds of 'uncommitted intimacy' (Moran and Hawisher 1998: 90) that talking to a screen can facilitate.

Combining comedy with the tradition of the epistolary novel, Matt Beaumont's *e* (2000) is composed entirely of the emails circulating amongst the employees of the fictional Miller Shanks advertising agency, employing graphic devices to convey the various ways in which the characters manipulate this sanctioned workplace communication tool to conduct their romantic affairs and spread gossip. Email is put to similar though much limited use in Helen Fielding's *Bridget Jones's Diary* (1996) as Bridget and Daniel clearly delight in subverting this still novel form of communication, as they play with the possibilities of combining office speak with flirtation and innuendo.

In the literature of the late 1980s and 1990s, technology is often closely linked to the exploration of issues of gender and sexuality, providing as it does ample new opportunities for disguise and identity play. A key literary text of the period engaging with issues of gender, identity and body politics in relation to new technologies is Jeanette Winterson's *The PowerBook* (2000), named after the Apple laptop whose branding helped move the technology away from its association with business, and to suggest continuities with older technologies such as that of the book. As well as using graphic icons to replicate the computer interface, Winterson's novel uses computer terminology for many of the chapter titles ('OPEN HARD DRIVE', 'EMPTY TRASH', 'RESTART'). While some references (e.g. to the Netscape Navigator) have quickly become dated, others (e.g. references to 'meatspace') connect with ongoing theoretical debates in cyberfeminism and posthumanism.

Winterson's novel clearly sets out to engage with the computer as a writing tool and to remediate some of the narrative techniques associated with hypertext fiction (discussed in Chapter 1). This was a deliberate attempt by Winterson to 'be part of what happens next' and to avoid becoming a mere 'curator in the Museum of Literature' (Winterson 2001). Other novelists who have responded to electronic literature, particularly interactive and multimodal forms, include Mark Z. Danielewski in *House of Leaves* (2000), and Jonathan Safran Foer in *Extremely Loud & Incredibly Close* (2005), which both experiment with the graphic surface of the text, multimodal effects and branching narrative structures (Gibbons 2012).

American novelists have perhaps tended to be more discomfited by technology and its potential impact on contemporary cultural life than their British counterparts. In her study of the American novel's 'anxiety of obsolescence' in the face of the growing dominance of television culture, Fitzpatrick (2006) argues that as well as resisting the perceived dehumanisation of the machine, one of the main anxieties expressed by contemporary writers concerns the loss of individuality that increasing mechanisation may bring. For example, Douglas Coupland's *Microserfs* (1996) incorporates email and chat room exchanges to the point where 'face talk' comes to seem something that has to be planned for and accommodated to. But while the virtual exchanges bring to the foreground the issues that many of the characters seem to have with intimacy and disclosing their innermost emotions, they are also evidence of their compulsion to keep seeking out opportunities for introspection and to make use the computer interface as a space for confession and unburdening (Thomas 2012).

Social media in the novel

Social media features in the contemporary novel both as a routine part of characters' everyday lives, and as a frustration or burden that they have to deal with in the context of managing their social lives. For example, in *The Whitstable High Tide Swimming Club* by Katie May, the women turn to social media to campaign for their club, even though they come to realise that this means a 'daily wade through the swamp of insults and abuse' (2018: 194) that accompany messages of solidarity. The novel also interestingly reflects on the different levels of engagement of the women: Maisie 'had been goaded' into joining Facebook and is 'mystified' (198) by what attracts people to it, and by the bad punctuation she finds in her friend Deb's posts. The novel follows Maisie's travels through social media as she browses the profiles of her fellow club members, checks out links to YouTube and finds herself being messaged by an old friend upset by her disappearance and seeming abandonment of her husband and her old life.

In some novels, rather than just providing a backdrop, social media may in fact define the central characters and their world. For example, *An Absolutely Remarkable Thing* (2018) by Hank Green explores the idea of internet celebrity through the central character of April May, while *Don't Call Me Baby* by Gwendolyn Heasley (2014) focuses on the experiences of the daughter of an internet blogger calling herself 'Mommylicious' as she turns to writing to try to reclaim her identity from that created for her by her mother. Aimed primarily at a young adult readership, these novels about social media influencers could be argued to constitute an evolving new genre, immersed not just in the practices but also the language of those caught up in a world where appearance and attention are everything.

Like email, Twitter can fairly easily be represented within a verbal art form such as the novel. In the latest Bridget Jones novel, *Bridget Jones: Mad About the Boy* (2013) Twitter fits readily into the diary format which characterises the series, though once again comic capital is derived from some of the faux pas Bridget commits as she learns to adapt to its affordances. Tweets and Facebook posts also feature in recent crime fiction, for example *Follow Me* by Angela Clarke (2015) and *Forward Slash* (2013) by Mark Edwards and Louise Voss. Here, social media is used as a shorthand for deviance and social networking platforms as spaces where serial killers can ensnare and track down their prey. Like email, novels featuring Twitter draw on the traditions of the epistolary novel and the diary form, and though writers may be at great pains to reproduce the distinctive affordances of the platform, reading tweets as part of an ongoing narrative does not disrupt the flow of the telling in the same way that reproducing a photograph or other visual representation might do. More difficult, too, is attempting to convey in prose fiction how users move between devices and platforms.

While this study is primarily interested in the ways in which forms of literary engagement and activity take place on or around social media, it is clearly instructive to also explore how the impact of social media is being dealt with and responded to within existing literary forms such as the novel. As social media has been such a talking point in recent years not always for the most positive of reasons, the fact that it is a subject that is of interest to novelists and others should come as no surprise, nor should the fact that in many cases the response is one of bemusement or disdain. However, I hope that this chapter has demonstrated how in so many ways social media brings exciting new opportunities for reigniting interest in existing forms of literature as well as new opportunities for creative engagement and play. Rather than see social media as a threat to the kinds of values of quality and depth associated with the literary, or assuming that users of social media cannot be knowledgeable about its traditions and conventions, examining the diverse forms that engagement can take must surely provide encouragement that mutual influence and renewed interaction will continue to thrive in these spaces.

3 The Twittersphere as literary playground

This chapter will provide an overview of 'born digital' literary works found on Twitter, including poetry and drama. The previous chapter has detailed how Twitter has been at the foreground of contemporary retellings and reimaginings of classic texts, and Chapter 5 will discuss some of the literary movements that have emerged across Twitter and other platforms. The focus of this chapter is primarily work that engages with and exploits the affordances of the platform, though in some cases I will discuss work that might easily have appeared in print or another medium but which relies for its subject matter and audience on what makes Twitter appealing and unique. My aim is to move discussion beyond the preoccupation with examples of literary outputs on Twitter as 'short bursts of beauty' (Franklin 2014), to examine whether Twitter can support more sustained and immersive forms.

Since my last study, which focused on Twitterfiction (Thomas 2016), a number of changes have taken place both in terms of the platform infrastructure, and in terms of how Twitter is perceived and valued culturally. Some of these changes were discussed in the Introduction, but of course may themselves have been overtaken by events by the time this book is published. In particular, far from being hailed as a driver of social change and champion of the marginalised, Twitter is now perceived negatively for the vitriol and toxicity of much of the discourse that takes place on the platform, and for providing little more than an empty echo chamber where the same content and opinions are endlessly being recirculated. As a direct consequence, many of the writers I included in my previous study have either left Twitter or disappeared from view.

Twitter as a platform for creativity

Despite some of these recent changes, Twitter is and remains the form of social media that I engage with most often. It is also the platform that has received most attention to date in terms of its literary outputs, though the emphasis has been primarily on storytelling and narrative, with much less discussion of drama or poetry. The fact that Twitter users are restricted to a limited number of characters (initially 140, now 280) may well have provided the spur or challenge for users to show their creativity. Moreover, the restrictions of the platform can easily be linked with those of already established literary forms such as the haiku, and with earlier examples of short form web-based writing such as the drabble or flash fiction (Thomas 2014a; Thomas 2016). As Goldsmith (2011) puts it, from the point of view of literary history, Twitter can be seen as but the latest in a long line of linguistic reductions.

Work developed in response to Twitter has appeared in print form (Aciman and Rensin 2009; Sreedharan 2014). In addition, several high-profile writers have turned to the platform to share work in progress or new writing, to create explore new imaginative worlds and to experiment with the affordances of the medium. Much attention (e.g. Andersen 2017) has been paid in particular to Jennifer Egan's short story 'Black Box' (2012), which followed previous experiments with embracing technology with an entire chapter from *A Visit from the Goon Squad* (2011) given over to a powerpoint presentation. Also much discussed was David Mitchell's use of Twitter in 2014 to publish a story in 300 tweets as an 'amuse bouche' for *The Bone Clocks* published later that year. While the experiment undoubtedly helped to publicise the novel, Mitchell's attempt at a Twitter story was roundly criticised by reviewers particularly because it did not appear to attempt to engage with or utilise the affordances of the platform or learn from burgeoning forms of Twitterliterature. In addition, the device of releasing the story to a strict timeline was criticised as having 'little clear narrative or stylistic benefit' (Crouch 2014). Critical reception for Mitchell's second story published on Twitter, '@I_Bombadil' was a bit more forgiving, recognising the 'steep learning curve' (Andersen 2017: 42) the author has gone through in terms of how comfortable he is using Twitter, particularly with regards to the use of multimodal elements, and also the references to current real world events. Undoubtedly, the fact that novelists are engaging with social media in this way points to its significance culturally. It also serves once again to demonstrate how the literary is experienced more and more across media and in interaction with popular cultural forms (Collins 2010).

These experiments have helped raise the profile of Twitterliterature, while also drawing parallels with literary history, for example Andersen's (2017) comparison of the 'staggered transmission' of content on Twitter with the serialisation of the Victorian novel. As further evidence of the cultural significance of this new writing, in 2012, an international online Twitterfiction festival was established to showcase work that 'uses Twitter functionality in the most creative way possible' and does 'something more than just tweeting out a narrative line-by-line'. Although the festival was fairly short lived (the last one was in 2015), it brought to prominence the range of work being generated by users of the platform, and started a process whereby these outputs could be evaluated and curated.

As already discussed in Chapter 2, Twitter provides ways for readers and fans to extend their engagement with characters or fictional worlds primarily encountered through film, tv or literary texts. In addition, the phenomenon of 'second screening', where users follow discussions on Twitter while watching a tv show or movie, not only extends engagement and allows for user participation, but can also contribute to eroding the boundaries between the real and the fictional (Lochrie and Coulton 2012). Similar activities can be observed in relation to readers discussing books using shared hashtags while Twitter has become a space where various literary events can be marked and shared (discussed further in Chapter 6). Moreover, the creativity in evidence on Twitter can be linked to the concept of the attention economy, as users not only have limited characters, but limited time to make their mark as their feeds and timelines are continually updating.

'Small stories' and the need for new methods and approaches

Like many other social media platforms, part of Twitter's function and appeal is built around the idea of users documenting their day to day activities. As a consequence, there has been considerable interest from linguists and narratologists in the 'small stories' found here and how these may challenge and subvert dominant narrative paradigms (discussed in the Introduction). Notably, Georgakopolou's (2007) work on the 'small stories' found on social media have demonstrated how retrospection and teleology, so important in traditional models of narrative, give way to breaking news and anticipation, fluidity and hybridity. Likewise, in her study of blogs and Facebook updates, Page (2011) argues that the episodic narratives found on social media do not fall readily into the traditional categories provided by narratologists. Studies of small stories tend to focus on news or narratives of the self (e.g. Thomas 2017) where the minutiae of daily life are shared so as to offer insights into a particular situation or condition. These can in turn be understood in the context of the kinds of 'vernacular creativity' (Burgess 2006) displayed across social media platforms where it is often the very rawness and lack of polish of the stories related that makes them so powerful. Although the place of fragmentary, ephemeral **life writing** practices in literary culture has been recognised, this has not yet fully been explored in relation to the memories and experiences daily shared on social media.

Despite the preoccupation with narrative and with providing close readings of Twitter texts, studies of storytelling and experimentation on Twitter have acknowledged the importance of attempting to capture the unique affordances of the platform, such as the experience of encountering the tweets as part of a timeline (Thomas 2014a; Thomas 2016), and the ways in which this may be closer to participating in a performance than to reading and responding to words on a page. Both Georgakopolou (2007) and Page (2010, 2012) have provided valuable critiques of the idea of narrative as a bounded unit, demonstrating instead the need to examine context and the situated practices associated with not just producing but sharing and responding to narratives. However, most narratological and linguistic studies of social media narratives still tend to focus on form, and to rely on traditional tools and methods in the analysis of the language of the narratives and the interactions that take place around them. In particular, there is a tendency to describe the linguistic features of social media posts and verbalised responses to them. Much less attention has been paid to the phenomenology of social media, for example analysing the unique contexts of reception for individual users, or paying attention to the unpredictable and uncontrollable circulation and recirculation of narratives across time and space. This kind of approach has traditionally been the preserve of media and cultural studies.

The emergence of Twitterfiction

As was mentioned in the last chapter, my first introduction to Twitter was primarily through spoof and parody accounts that created a sense of playfulness but also displayed creativity and ingenuity in exploiting the affordances of the medium. But it was an article by Yourgrau (2009) tracing Twitterfiction to Japanese cellphone fictions ('keitai shosetsu') that suggested to me that Twitter could offer something more sustained in terms of characterisation and plotting, and an experience that could be talked about and shared on a different level to that of enjoying the humour of the parody accounts. It was this article, that I shared at the time with colleague Chindu Sreedharan, that became the inspiration for his retelling of the Mahabharata on Twitter via @epicretold (see Chapter 2 and Thomas 2014a; Thomas 2016).

Yourgrau's article particularly focused on the potential of Twitter to accommodate ongoing narratives and drew attention to one of the earliest examples of what became known as Twitterfiction, namely *New York Times* journalist Matt Richtel's real-time thriller, the 'Twiller'. First appearing on Twitter in 2008, Richtel's narrative, described by him (cited by Yourgrau 2009) as a kind of 'Memento on a mobile' (referring to the film of that name) recounted the story of a man who wakes up with amnesia fearing he may be a murderer. What Richtel (2008) called his 'experiment in a new medium' confused many people, leading the author to confess that 'I don't know if the story will catch much attention, but, then again, it doesn't require much attention at all'. Yet Richtel's story demonstrated that readers would return again and again to pick up the threads of a well-told tale, or what Goldsmith calls the 'slow accumulation of tiny shards' (2011: 177). It also provided an early demonstration that Twitterfiction could capture the attention of a wide range of users, including cultural commentators and critics.

Since Richtel's *Twiller*, crime stories and thrillers have continued to prove popular particularly for narrative formats that use social media or instant messaging to 'cross over into our daily lives' (Walker 2004). For example, storytelling app Unrd's *Last Seen Online,* a 'fiction for the Whatsapp generation' (Flatt 2017) invited users to try to work out what happened to a missing girl based on her last known messages. Particularly with time-bound narratives such as *Last Seen Online* and *Hurst* (discussed by Thomas 2016), the experience of following the main character's ever more frantic tweets is both disconcerting and highly immersive, as is evident from responses to the narratives from users. I have argued previously that this results in a 'narrative experience where users are not only followers of the story, but are in turn followed by that story' (Thomas 2016: 365), and indeed feature as actors in the staging of events. Relying on serialisation and pacing of the narrative to provide readers with the sense of an unfolding narrative (and increased threat for the protagonists), these stagings are able to build an immersive story facilitated by the fact that Twitter, unlike Facebook, allows users to create fictional accounts. Although there is clearly a potential for deception, such narratives can promote a similar kind of 'sincere engagement' to that Ondrak (2018: 164) observes in relation to the creepypasta phenomenon (discussed in the previous chapter), as participants play along with or improvise material in ways crucial to the story's effectiveness but also symptomatic of the 'merging of "real" and "textual life"' (Ondrak 2018: 166) characteristic of the social media age.

Levey (2016) has argued that 'post-press literature' has brought renewed interest in serial forms of literature that benefit both authors and readers in terms of cost and enhanced sociality. I have previously written about how Sreedharan engaged in an ongoing dialogue with followers of @epicretold over the course of its production, even dedicating the print version of the text to those 'who forced me to finish what I began' (Sreedharan 2014). I have also argued (Thomas 2014a; Thomas 2016) that this kind of interaction necessitates that any analysis of literary outputs on social media and especially Twitter, needs to go beyond discussion of language and aesthetics to account for the ways in which followers not only take up and disseminate those outputs but contribute to their development. Twitter provides many of the tools which can make this kind of analysis easier, providing numerical records of likes and retweets at a glance, while also making it possible for users to save and share discussions and threads.

Nevertheless, despite early experiments with serialisation, it has been the challenges of telling a story within 140/280 characters that dominate discussions of Twitterfiction. Antecedents for this kind of writing can be found not only in Japanese cellphone fiction or 'thumb novels', but in the 100 word 'drabble' from fan cultures, and flashfiction, a form which has produced its own competitions, awards, and even its own 'National Day'. In his study of contemporary forms of 'microfiction', Nelles (2012) reminds us that 'there have always been artists willing to risk the miniature' going back as far as ancient forms such as the parable and the fable. Yet Twitter's seeming constraints appear to have provided added impetus for users to seek out ever more innovative workarounds and ways of standing out from the busy flow of information with which they have to compete. Twitter is thus well placed to allow for a certain degree of experimentation for writers who may be inspired (for example the Alt Lit poets discussed in Chapter 5) by the radical aleatory experiments of the 'cut-up' technique made famous by William Burroughs and others in the 1960s, teasing readers with fragments that hold out the promise of some kind of meaningful connection, but at the same time challenging the very idea that meaning can be predicted or consciously controlled. Meanwhile, David Mitchell (Poole 2014) has acknowledged that his attempt to write for Twitter was inspired by the Oulipo (Ouvroir de littérature potentielle) movement in France in the 1960s and its explorations of the 'potential' of literary writing working against the constraints of language and form (discussed in Chapter 1).

Experiments with automation

As discussed in Chapter 2, social media has provided a space for experimentation with algorithms and with artificial intelligence, as in the case of @shelley_ai, where 'Shelley' is 'raised' on eerie stories from reddit to feed her 'creepy creative mind' (https://www.media.mit.edu/projects/shelley/overview/) but also so that 'she' can collaborate with humans. Elsewhere, too, human interactions with operating systems have inspired creative responses, for example 'SIRI & Me' (2013) by Esmerelda Kosmatopoulos based on screenshots of texts between Siri and the author, and *Siri & Me: A Modern Love Story* (2012), a series of cartoons by David Milgrim. New materialism and Actor Network Theory (discussed in the Introduction) help to provide a context for these new kinds of negotiation with the non-human and with the idea of agency in relation to the 'artificial'. They are also instructive in highlighting our continued reliance on anthropomorphic frames of reference.

The fact that Twitter is dominated by text has led to its infiltration by various kinds of bots producing automated posts from found text. For example @pentametron, based in 'Stratford-upon-Internet' retweets content that conforms to the iambic pentameter (Good morning thankful for another day; I've never witnessed such a lovely sight), playing on the clash between the seeming banality of the utterances and their (re)presentation in the context of a literary form associated with Shakespeare and the highest traditions of poetry. Elsewhere, the surreality and ambiguity over authorship and meaning that algorithmic tweets produce has inspired some high-profile experiments, including @horse_ebooks, which gained notoriety when it emerged that the spambot was in fact a performance art piece.

@MagicRealismBot tweets stories every two hours inspired by Borges' 'hyperteleological' creations (Rodley 2015), where an underlying structure or principle is repeated and exaggerated ad absurdum. Although @MagicRealismBot is managed by a team which includes a coder, the Australian-based digital author and academic Chris Rodley is the driving force behind the account. @MagicRealismBot relies on intimate knowledge and understanding of the genre, but it is the ambiguity about the extent to which the tweets are random or cleverly contrived that provides part of the pleasure of following the account. For example, 'A prime minister floats on a lake filled with yoghurt' (posted on 4 August 2018) could be interpreted as a very apposite commentary on the situation of UK Prime Minister Theresa May at the time, embroiled as she was in the whole Brexit crisis. With its mix of fantastical and real settings, and its repetition of grammatical structures, @MagicRealismBot plays with the idea of variations on a theme, but with a nod to the knowing reader familiar with the genre and its political and cultural underpinnings.

Expressionism Bot (@Trakl_Bot), like @MagicRealismBot, was set up as a 'poetic experiment' by a team comprising an academic, a writer and a coder. The aim of the account is to 'generate Expressionist images – sublime and ridiculous' (see Fig 3.1). Like @MagicRealismBot, too, certain grammatical constructions recur offering followers a daily dose of evocative images generated to emulate the work of the literary movement from the early twentieth century. As with the experiments with hypertext and automatic writing discussed in Chapter 1, these accounts consciously draw on and play with literary concepts and antecedents as

Expressionism Bot @Trakl_Bot   Oct 20
I dance God's death

Figure 3.1 Expressionism Bot

much for theoretical exploration as for creative expression. But the numbers of followers for these accounts (especially @MagicRealismBot) suggests a much greater degree of success in terms of attracting and sustaining an audience.

'Nowness' and liminality

According to Goldsmith (2011) one of the consequences of the kind of compression of language that we find on Twitter is an augmented sense of urgency. Alongside the limit on characters, one of the other distinctive features of Twitter is its reverse chronology, meaning that the latest tweets appear first in the user's timeline, creating what Page has termed its characteristic 'pull of the present' (Page 2012: 13). Twitter clients provide users with the means to see which are the current 'trending topics' while hashtags allow users to easily **tag** and share content and thus help drive what is trending. The social and 'live' aspects of Twitter as a storytelling environment therefore provide new opportunities for tracking how stories unfold, and how readers respond to narratives told in real time. They also raise many issues to do with who controls the narrative, and suggests that reception may be much more complex and multi-layered than is the case with accounts of the experience of reading or viewing discrete texts undistracted. The possibility of linking outwards to other content, and the creation of multiple connected accounts further allow for the creation of a sense of a 'multidimensional realtime' (Vlieghe, Page and Rutten 2016) of a rich and involving kind. As narrative tweets appear in our timelines alongside all the other news and chatter that fills the Twittersphere, the effect can be jarring, much as in instances of metalepsis or 'breaking the frame' in print fiction, where the sense of reality that has been set up in a narrative is disrupted by some kind of intrusion, for example by the real world figure of the author. However, as well as having the potential to shock or terrify, the effect can be highly exhilarating and thrilling, creating for users the sense that they are part of a story whose outcomes may be unpredictable or improvised according to how circumstances unfold. The experience being offered to followers is thus imbued with a 'strong sense of potentiality' (Kozel 2014) gathering momentum as more and more followers join in and return time and time again to see how things turn out.

Margolin (1999) has argued that contemporary culture is characterised by a preference for stories that relate not what has happened, but what is happening, and that place the emphasis on telling the story 'as you live'. This is nowhere more evident than on Twitter with its constant reiteration of the need to update in 'real time'. Also drawing on narratological terms and theories, Mäkelä (2019) sees parallels between social media forms and literary tropes and techniques, especially present tense narration and epistolary fictions, arguing that the shared focus on experientiality and simultaneity places the emphasis on immediacy and inwardness in terms of the stories told.

Meanwhile, John Fiske's (1987) concept of 'nowness' in television has been extended to the analysis of cross-platform viewing and fan cultures in the digital age as well as to social media (Thomas 2011a; Page 2012). In his account of the 'nowness' of television, Fiske argues that the phenomenon is not confined to live programming, but is something that can accrue over time for viewers who return to the same locations and characters over periods of months and years, leading to a kind of engagement and affective bond that can be powerful. Retellings of familiar tales such as the Mahabharata by @epicretold (discussed in Chapter 2 and by Thomas 2016) can therefore conjure a sense of 'nowness' for their followers, while Twitter is also able to stage storytelling events that offer users something much closer to a 'live' experience.

Mobile platforms and instant messaging have been used as a way to play with these boundaries in ways that can be both exhilarating and unsettling. For example, Blast Theory's *Karen* (https://www.blasttheory.

co.uk/projects/karen/) created in 2015, offered users their very own life coach and personalised experience, but one with a strong narrative trajectory focused on the life coach's own life problems. Like other narratives designed for mobile and cross-platform consumption, with Twitterfiction 'the distinctions drawn between inside the story and outside the story take on a new kind of fluidity' (Goggin and Hamilton 2014: 231). Twitter narratives often blur the boundaries between the real and the fictional, both to offer social commentary on news or political events, and to engender in readers the feeling that they need to keep up with the story and that their participation is not just desired but necessary.

One of the most celebrated of Twitter writers, Nigerian-American writer, journalist and photographer Teju Cole used the platform mainly to share creative nonfiction and commentaries on social and political issues of the day. Between 2011 and 2013, Cole developed his own distinctive form of Twitterfiction, the 'small fate', based on the French literary *fait divers*, which he translated on his website (n.d) as 'news of the weird'. Cole further defines the form as featuring 'an event, usually of a grim nature, animated sometimes, but not always, by a certain irony'.

In addition to defining his own form of Twitter writing, Cole's reflections on Twitter as a new platform for literature are often insightful, for example his account of his realisation that 'That's where the people are, so bring the literature to them right where they are' (cited by Pearce 2011). He also demonstrates his knowledge and understanding of the platform's affordances, notably Twitter's ability to allow him to 'put something into people's day' (cited by Zhang 2013) in a way that may be provocative or unsettling. For instance, in 'Seven short stories about drones', published on Twitter in 2013, he inserts news of the devastating consequences of drone strikes into a series of tweets featuring the opening lines from landmark literary texts such as Virginia Woolf's *Mrs Dalloway* and Chinua Achebe's *Things Fall Apart*.

In one of his most experimental works, 'Hafiz', a story about a man found lying in the street, is recounted via thirty-one retweets from thirty-one different Twitter accounts. Cole describes the decision to tell the story via retweets as 'an occasion for grace, for doing something unusual together' (cited by Vecsey 2014), drawing attention to the phenomenon of retweeting and 'how you can make someone else present in your timeline' while at the same time creating a collaborative storytelling situation capable of being experienced in many different ways by users. 'Hafiz' could be accessed in its entirety as orchestrated by Cole on his Twitter feed, and repetition and echoing help to create a strong choral effect. Nevertheless, followers of the individual real-life accounts of the retweeters might only ever encounter single tweets and perspectives, providing multiple points of entry for readers, and facilitating a distributed narrative experience (Walker 2004) which both challenges and rewards.

Cole has not posted to his Twitter account since 2014, and on his website he refers only to the fact that 'I was active on Twitter, but not anymore'. He remains active on Facebook (for news of appearances and so on) and Instagram, where he 'posts photographs and thinks about images by others'.

Distribution

Many of the examples of Twitterfiction discussed so far connect out-wards, whether that is to a pre-existing text, an author's website, or other networks and sharing services such as Instagram or YouTube. This adds again to the sense of narrative as something that is distributed across platforms and networks (Walker 2004), and as something that readers and followers can participate in by distributing to their net-works. In his study of the Twitter feed for the launch of role-playing videogame *Mass Effect 3*, Holmes (2013) argues that the story arc, pro-duced in real time 'as if' the story were taking place in the real world, relied on the fact that Twitter was 'enmeshed with the everyday stream of other writing and reading' that entered into the real world of the reader. According to Holmes, it is the fact that readers experience events 'as if' real that motivates them to participate by creating supplemental stories as well as interacting with other readers.

With these kinds of cross-platform, improvisatory and immersive narratives, the staging of the user experience and the role of the user as a potential performer make it difficult to define where the boundaries might lie between narrative and drama, authors and directors and read-ers and performers. Experimentation is thus much more about exploring these liminal spaces and providing followers with the experience of 'now-ness' than about creating a fictional text or artefact that can be revisited or stored, making it difficult for such work to receive close critical attention after the event.

Genre and audience

Alongside the impulse to experiment and test the limits of a platform such as Twitter, it is important to acknowledge that the idea of 'following' par-ticular accounts over time also creates a culture where repetition and familiarity may be highly valued. Genre fiction continues to proliferate on the platform, providing readers with recognisable patterns and conventions from Gothic horror (@VeryShortStory) or science fiction (@jeffnoon). The focus in these fictions is often on action and outlandish or extreme events rather than character development or relationships.

In 2008, Canadian author Arjun Basu began composing what he called 'twisters' (short stories told on Twitter), posting at least one tweet a day, usually featuring relationship mishaps affecting an unnamed 'he' and 'she':

> He wears his success with a mixture of pride and self loathing. She sniffs the air and makes a face. I know, he sighs, stroking his billfold. (27 January 2016)

Attracting hundreds of thousands of followers and featuring in early studies of Twitterfiction (Thomas 2014a, 2016), Basu provided his readers with a daily 'fix' of these short tales based on set themes perfect for reading on the go. However, in February of 2018 Basu announced on his blog that 'the Twisters are over', blaming the doubling of the character limit but also the proliferation of hate speech on the platform. Basu credits giving up on the Twister with increasing his productivity (he is now the author of two novels) and helping him rediscover the joys of television.

Like Basu, @MicroFlashFic promises followers a regular stream of stories but 'of every kind' (17 October 2018). Potential followers can even sample a 'collection' of tweets 'to help you decide if this account is for you' (17 October 2018). Also reminiscent of Basu, the stories focus on the everyday and on seemingly inconsequential conversations between unnamed characters. Variation is provided by, for example, having stories composed entirely of dialogue:

> "I'm getting better at this adulting thing."
> "Oh?"
> "Last night I was eating a cookie in the bathroom. Part of it broke off and hit the floor. And I just threw it away."
> "What kind of cookie?"
> "Oatmeal chocolate chip."
> "I don't say this often, but you're a better person than me."
> (16 October 2018)

The account also offers variety in terms of having named characters in some of the stories and occasionally embedding photographs or other images.

@terriblytiny is another account which publishes stories daily from a 'diverse pool of creative writers'. Based in Mumbai, India, and describing itself as 'the world's most celebrated micro-fiction platform', it claims to have a readership of over 12 million per week and has its own merchandise based on the distinctive 'ttt' brand. The stories have been celebrated by Bhandara (2017) as offering a fresh and distinctive insight into aspects of contemporary life in India, particularly issues around gender and religion as in the following story named #Cover:

"Cover your head!"
her father insisted.
She ran inside.
Came back with her helmet.
Jenai Dalal (@terriblytiny 22 October 2015)

However, arguably one of the most distinctive features of the tiny tales is their poignancy and appeal to the emotions, often set against the stresses and pressures of the technological age:

In this age of screens and keyboards
I have missed writing so many beautiful
words on paper
And I don't want your name to be one of
them.
Divyanshi Vyas (@terriblytiny 24 October 2018)

In the context of the vast amount of information and accounts competing for our attention on Twitter, accounts that promise users something familiar and reliable to return to can have a strong appeal. This can extend to scheduled activities that take place at regular times, for example #LossLit's Twitter 'writeclub' which takes place every first Wednesday of the month (between 9 and 11 p.m. GMT). Though the hashtag can be used at other times to compose and share responses to the idea of loss, this scheduled activity leads to heightened visibility as well as helping to create a strong sense of community for participants, many of whom post several times during the allotted time frame. Again, the focus is often on the everyday and conjuring images ('a leaky biro') that evoke very personal expressions of grief or loss but in such a way that the follower can easily relate to:

I still have your chapstick in the
pocket of the jacket you loaned me.
It smells of lint, a leaky biro, beer, and
a dozen kisses we almost had
without laughing #LossLit
(@angelreadman 7 November 2018)

In evaluating the impact of these tweets, therefore, it is important to recognise how the shared hashtag invites the follower to see them as responses to one another as much as to the shared theme or focus. Other groupings formed on Twitter, for example @myhaikupond may be based on a shared interest in a particular form rather than a theme, but likewise an individual tweet or individual account can reach new audiences while also fostering a strong sense of community among users (discussed further in Chapter 5).

Poetry and performance

The focus on 'nowness' and constant updating that we find on platforms such as Twitter and Facebook raises questions to do with performativity. Removed from the timeline and from the particular moment that they may be seeking to reflect, it can be difficult to understand the impact of tweets and their significance for followers. This extends to the relationship between the writer or poet and his or her audience and the expectation users have of an instantaneous response or ongoing dialogue. Most evident with time-bound stories or events (for example *Hurst*, discussed in Thomas 2016), where access to a tweet or a thread may actually be restricted or completely removed, the performativity can further be found in the focus on topical or breaking events, and in the ways in which the writer/poet/performer signals to the follower that the 'work' is ephemeral or requires his or her input.

Chapter 5 provides discussion of the phenomenon of the Instapoet, and focuses on the role of poetry and the poet in contemporary literary movements particularly associated with or derived from social media. On Twitter, as will be discussed further in Chapter 6, established poets such as Ian McMillan and Lemn Sissay regularly interact with their followers, at the same time as sharing existing and new work.

However, the title the 'Poet Laureate of Twitter' has been reserved for Brian Bilston, described in the print edition of his work as 'a poet clouded in the pipe smoke of mystery' who has attracted large following of 'Bilstons' (57k as of 18 October 2018) since he first began publishing his poems under the pseudonym on Twitter in 2013. In the Introduction to the collection of poems published by the **crowdfunding** publisher Unbound (discussed in Chapter 6), Bilston is self-deprecating about his abilities as a poet ('There *are* pieces in here which I am not even sure are poems'). Rather than craft and technical prowess, Bilston claims that his poetry is 'composed when I was in the middle of these situations', driven by his belief that 'there is poetry to be found in anything if you look hard enough' (Bilston 2016).

Bilston's poetry frequently makes reference to the features and affordances of social media, for example in 'The Day That Twitter went Down' (2016) or 'A Brief History of the #' (26 August 2017). Moreover, in an edited version of an appearance on Radio 4 (BBC News Magazine 2016), he describes what he does as providing 'an opportunity for poetry to present itself in situations where and when people most need it', demonstrating his sensitivity to what brings people to social media and keeps them engaged with the accounts they follow. However, the poems tend to be inserted complete into the timeline rather than shared as tweets, so it could be argued that Bilston is more of a Poet Laureate *on* rather than *of* Twitter in the sense of exploiting or responding to its affordances. He clearly sees his role as a Twitter poet to provide his followers with a 'deeper engagement with real world concerns' as he responds to news events ('The White House' 22 August 2017), and contemporary social issues ('Refugees', 2016). Nevertheless, his outputs include pieces based on traditional poetic forms (especially the haiku) and poems engaging with popular culture and the simple pleasures in life ('Cuppa'). Unlike the Instagram poets whom I will discuss later, Bilston's cultural references ('Subbuteo', 'University Challenged', various poems dedicated to the singer Morrissey), suggest his primary audience is British, middle aged and middle class. Performativity here can be observed in the way in which the persona is cultivated but also engaged with by users – Bilston maintains a constant dialogue with followers 'in character' and they often playfully tease him about weak rhymes or try to get him to reveal information about himself ('I hope you are a Libra Brian').

As discussed in the previous chapter, a key question with the forms of Twitterliterature discussed above is whether they offer any innovation beyond fitting content around a new container. In some cases, for example the work of Brian Bilston, it appears that the content produced on Twitter can easily be exported to another medium, as with the print collection *You Took the Last Bus Home* (Bilston 2016), ensuring that the work is preserved but additionally allowing it to reach new audiences.

The culture of Twitter, with its focus on following particular accounts, retweeting and liking posts means that a focus purely on the content of an individual tweet provides only a very superficial insight into how that tweet may be experienced by followers at a given time, or how it is taken up and shared by users across time. This presents a challenge to traditional literary criticism, which may talk about context and milieu, but which has been slow to fully engage with empirical or ethnographic work based on reader or audience response. Even less common are studies which combine this kind of analysis with attention to infrastructure and modes of production, and yet this is precisely what I would argue is needed to move studies of social media literature beyond sterile debates about quality to begin to understand how these works impact on users, and how those same users take up, reimagine and relocate them to further extend their reach.

Chapter 5 will return to the question of whether or not literary forms and movements emerging on social media can be classed as 'literary' particularly if that definition depends on notions of lasting value, innovation or complexity. This chapter has provided some evidence to support the suggestion that social media may be more of a playground or training ground for writers than a space they want to stay in and develop. Perhaps it is true that writers like Basu and Cole are, as Levey (2016) puts it, 'holding out for traditional validation' and move on (or back) to print and traditional publishing models to ensure that they benefit economically and reputationally from their writing. Chapter 6 will consider how prizes and awards, new publishing platforms and access to literary advice may help social media writers to attain a sense of distinction and develop their skills.

Despite the fact that key figures such as Cole and Basu have deserted the platform, arguably Twitter offers us the closest approximation so far in terms of offering a glimpse of the new kind of literature that may emerge from social media understood in terms of a distinctive body of work, with shared conventions and features but also shared practices in terms of uptake and response. In addition, arguably like many previous literary movements and particularly the concept of literary defamiliarisation, as Goldsmith (2011: 175) contends, if nothing else 'the interface of Twitter has reframed ordinary language to make it extraordinary'. Moreover, as was mentioned in Chapter 2, the fact that it is mainly a platform for sharing text makes it especially amenable to being remediated in print form, as well as making it amenable to the kind of close reading traditionally associated with the study of literature and to the kinds of curation and canonisation discussed in the next chapter.

4 Canons and curators: accessing, preserving and evaluating the literary on social media

This chapter will address issues arising from the curation of literary content found on social media and the extent to which works may emerge which require the preservation and/or close critical attention associated with canonisation. The chapter will outline some of the tools and methods developed within the field of digital humanities to provide 'big data' analyses of cultural trends and shifts, as well as for archiving and preserving digital content. It will additionally consider how online communities and fan cultures have produced their own systems for categorising and organising material, and for ensuring that content is discoverable and free to access.

The previous chapter provided some insights into the kinds of literary content found on social media, and some of the ways in which that content is shared, disseminated and customised by users. Throughout this study, I have argued that the distinction between content creators and users is frequently blurred in online environments where texts are constantly being updated and modified, recirculated across different platforms and accessed at different times, and on different devices with their own unique affordances.

As ever, it is dangerous to overstate the novelty or uniqueness of these emerging trends. The RED (Reading Experience Database https://www. open.ac.uk/Arts/reading/) project provides ample evidence of the ways in which readers have always played a role in archiving and curating their reading, whether through providing catalogues of books for wills, or keeping journals accounting for books acquired and/or books read. In other fields, too, amateur or lay curation has a long history, especially where the objects may not always have had the kind of cultural prestige that makes curation or archiving more routine, for example comics. In fan cultures the labour required for preserving, cataloguing and rating fan produced fiction, art and video has long been recognised (Jenkins 1992; Stanfill and Condis 2014). In particular, Jenkins's (2006b) rearticulation of Lévy's (1997) concept of 'collective intelligence' attempts to account for the ways in which fans work together and pool their resources to try to decipher plot holes or to build a kind of database of knowledge about a particular text world. Within fan communities, too, the roles of administrators and moderators may be recognised and highly valued (Thomas and Round 2016). Such activities help to foster a sense of ownership and investment both in the fan texts and in the community, though, as will be discussed further in the next chapter, not without the possibility of tensions and hierarchies emerging between users.

The curatorial turn

Despite this long history, writer and digital publisher Michael Bhaskar (2016) has argued that curation has become a highly valued and much needed role in a world where we are often overwhelmed by the sheer volume of data that comes with our most routine of daily activities. He further examines how new forms of machine-driven curation are now commonly used by global corporations such as Apple and Amazon to provide customers with choices tailored to their specific requirements. Bhaskar's study pays far less attention to the kinds of online curation fans undertake, and he is rather sweeping in describing pre-internet fandoms as characterised by a kind of devotion absent from the 'few clicks away' (285) forms of identification and allegiance facilitated by the internet. Bhaskar contends that curation has lower barriers to participation than creation, and he sees the 'miracle' of access to information as something that has quickly become a 'problem'. Nevertheless, the study is important in raising the profile of curation in the contemporary context, and in foregrounding the activities of selecting, finding and cutting down that we all participate in, even if we might disagree that this inevitably brings us to a shared sense of 'what matters' (3).

One of the main motivations for Bhaskar's study is to retrieve the sense of custodianship and care that he feels is missing from some contemporary versions of curation. In particular, instead of the 'superstar' curators who are able to successfully navigate and harness new technologies, Bhaskar seems to hark back to a time when curators could be relied on for expertise and good judgement. In the case of literature, this inevitably ties in to notions of taste, quality and the kind of gatekeeping which may shore up rather than dismantle barriers. It also perhaps relates to debates about the extent to which notions of canonicity may apply in a context where texts are ephemeral and where the roles of gatekeepers and cultural intermediaries are more fluid and contested.

In the field of communication and marketing, scholars have written about the 'curatorial logic' of social media, focusing in particular on social media 'influencers' (Bolat and Gilani 2018) and how they manage their social relations with followers and accrue reputational capital. Moreover, Bolat and Gilani discuss how influencers curate others' skills and knowledge and curate infrastructure by learning more about how the platform is used by others and about the particular conventions that may apply to the specific kind of blog or activity they are engaged in.

New kinds of curation may develop alongside new platforms and practices. In her study of Snapchat, Walker Rettberg (2018) refers to the fact that the kind of archiving common to Twitter and Facebook only occurs on Snapchat when attempts are made to create collective narratives ('Our Stories') curated not by users but by production managers. This may perhaps also be explained by the fact that newer varieties of social media such as Snapchat have emerged in the context of cloud computing and live streaming, fundamentally unsettling how we might traditionally conceive of archiving, storing and categorising content.

The activity of 'lifestreaming', defined by Wargo (2015: 560) as 'a rhetorical act of streaming documents, texts, and visuals to curate an imagined and real self' is an activity, like the 'selfie', which is primarily associated with young people. Rather than dismiss this activity as narcissism as so many do, Wargo (2015) argues that it is a highly literate and rhetorical practice productive of a 'myriad of selves' (561) drawing on 'sedimented identity texts' that 'stitch together divides of space and place and bifurcations such as online/offline' (567). Such practices also have to be understood in the context of the kind of vast and instant archives digitisation has made possible, and as a response to the constant threat of obsolescence in a contemporary media landscape where apps and platforms constantly come and go.

Canons and fanons

The idea of the canon as it applies to literature has been roundly challenged by feminists and postcolonial theorists amongst others. Debates about canonicity have also been prompted by electronic and web-based literatures that bring into question traditional notions of how we measure literary worth and value. For example, Bolter in *Writing Space* (2001) asks whether the whole idea of the canon is a relic of print culture, difficult if not impossible to apply to the network cultures emerging in online spaces. He links this to growing scepticism about the extent to which high culture functions as a unifying rather than divisive force, locating these challenges not just in terms of technological change, but in relation to postmodern aesthetics.

Ensslin's *Canonizing Hypertext* (2007) specifically focused on the extent to which the idea of the canon can be used in relation to hypertext fiction. The study both examines a range of hypertext fictions as literary texts that could potentially be accepted into an existing literary canon, and sets out to explore whether hypertext fiction can be said to have formed its own distinctive canon. Although Ensslin moves towards a concept of canon that is more focused on creativity and openness than closed or restrictive models, she returns to the idea of canon as a force that can bind cultures together and foster a sense of belonging, and as something that is collaboratively achieved rather than imposed from outside. The main motivations for this endeavour to reclaim the notion of canon are to establish why and how these new kinds of fiction can be studied and evaluated, and how they may be incorporated into existing literary curricula.

For the creators of new media and electronic texts, canonisation may be more about facilitating preservation and discoverability than ascribing value. As discussed in Chapter 1, the Electronic Literature Organization has created its own collaborative online knowledge base to document and map the 'ongoing' field of electronic literature. Related projects include 'Rebooting Electronic Literature', which sets out to document pre-web born digital media and an initiative begun in 2018 and supported by the Andrew W. Mellon Foundation to migrate the ELO's existing archives to an open-source repository to ensure their preservation and improve accessibility. In the case of the ELO initiatives, those charged with selecting and preserving texts are themselves either actively involved in creating electronic literature, or are scholars dedicated to its study. To some extent, this is therefore a closed community, but the sense that the work is generated by and for a community is strong, and many of those involved provide their expertise and labour for free.

In the context of online communities and fan cultures, alternative notions of the canon have emerged in relation to works that themselves derive from pre-existing texts and fictional universes. So in fanfiction communities, canon may refer to which texts can be included, for example where a particular franchise has multiple adaptations, reboots and paratexts that could potentially be included. It also refers to the details of that fictional universe, including characterisation and plot, which are taken as fixed points from which departures and variations can be located. Thus fanfiction writers will often categorise their stories according to how far they follow the canon or depart from it, for example explicitly labelling stories Out of Character (OOC) where the characters they write about radically depart from those in the canon. The term '**fanon**' (fan canon) has emerged (Thomas 2007a) to account for the ways in which certain tropes become widely accepted in a particular fandom. Fanon can become 'canon' when the creators of the pre-existing texts take up and use those tropes, for example where details about a character's past, or their preferences and predilections are incorporated into the characterisation by the makers of the tv show, film or video game.

Curating the everyday

YouTube's slogan for many years was 'Broadcast Yourself', encouraging users to record their everyday activities no matter how trivial. The emphasis today is much more on 'voice' and the freedom to express oneself than on display or performance. Users can create their own 'channels' as well as tagging and sharing videos made by themselves or others. Users can additionally mark videos to 'watch later', create play-lists, save 'liked videos' and review their 'watch history'. The site also filters content for viewers so that they can choose to watch videos posted in the last hour, or last week, select features including live or 3D, or choose videos by location. YouTube is home to many book vloggers and book clubs, as well as the fan 'vid' where users can create homages to favourite authors, texts or characters, and the 'mash up' where content from more than one source is 'mashed' together to produce a new work. Jane Austen mashups on YouTube include several examples mashing scenes from various film adaptations of the novels, while Harry Potter fans have mashed scenes from the films with contemporary pop videos (e.g. by Taylor Swift) as well as mashups with other high profile literary franchises (Lord of the Rings). Since 2012, the **BookTube** community has had its own channel with just under 5,000 subscribers (as of 11 December 2018), offering advice for writers as well as discussions about book-related topics.

Services such as Flickr, Instagram and Pinterest allow users to curate content for others to share with a strong emphasis on the visual and on the aesthetics of the ways in which the content is framed. Flickr and Instagram allow users to collate photographs around memories or stories that can be shared with others, while Pinterest places the emphasis on 'discovery' and 'ideas', often based on crafts, hobbies or projects that users want to display, sometimes with a view to getting feedback and new ideas. According to some sources, as much as 71% of Pinterest's user base is female, and it is often linked to traditionally female collective activities such as quilting or collage.

'Discovery' and 'love' are prominently featured on Tumblr's sign-in page (https://www.tumblr.com, as of August 2019), with a strong emphasis on ease of use ('really, really simple') and on the wide range of content ('literally whatever') that can be incorporated into the blog format. In this context, the 'random' is not viewed pejoratively but positively, as is the idea of appropriating content and recirculating it: 'See something great? Reblog it to your own blog... Make it your own', justified on the basis that 'Other people will do the same with your posts' and that 'That's how you meet people here'. The language of the site is all about inclusivity and reassurance ('You already know how this works'; 'Come on in'), however, in addition creativity features prominently with Content being defined as 'creative expression' and with reference to what users post as a 'work' or a 'creation' (Terms, June 2018). Tumblr's embrace of appropriation and recycling has led to concerns over privacy and intellectual property. Likewise, in fan cultures Tumblr has become a hugely popular and important platform, but one where the very freedoms it offers are seen to lead to new kinds of 'toxic' practices (Hills 2018), especially abuse and hate speech directed towards vulnerable individuals.

Although Tumblr has received relatively little scholarly attention compared to other social media, Munteanu has described it as an 'ideal "curatorial" platform' which provides users with a 'collaborative (trans) personal/(trans) media archival space' (2017: 126, 148). Munteanu goes on to argue that the kinds of personal expression made possible on Tumblr differ from those afforded by predominantly text-based platforms such as Twitter.

Meanwhile, Stein (2016) has argued that Tumblr's interface, particularly the 'infinite scrolling' it facilitates, helps convey a sensation of limitlessness which is particularly attuned to fan cultures and their endless pursuit of 'more of' and 'more from' the objects of their devotion (Pugh 2005). Stein contradicts the platform's own emphasis on how intuitive its use is, arguing that it can seem opaque and impenetrable to new users. However, she further argues that its 'emphasis on multiplicitous plenitude' produces its own aesthetic forms. Among these, Williams (2018) lists the gifset (collection or set of **gif** images) and the fanmix (compilation of e.g. songs inspired by the source text), both of which rely on selection and combination. Williams draws on Stein's article to articulate her own experience of using Tumblr as a means of working through trauma and mourning, allowing her to derive comfort from revisiting content through the constant looping and repetition that the platforms makes possible. She claims that its opacity and impenetrability offers a space for lone fans, while the fact that Tumblr allows for posts of varying lengths makes possible work that is very detailed and in depth.

In a study of transmedia literacy amongst teenagers across Australia, South America and Europe, Scolari (2018) draws attention to the particular skill sets involved not only in adapting to new interfaces or the affordances of different platforms, but also in building relationships, communities, and managing content, including the presentation of the self and one's social relations. In addition, the study argues that users acquire skills in identifying and evaluating potential risks. So, as outlined earlier, while Tumblr has not been without its own controversies and 'wars', advice and coping mechanisms are readily developed, deployed and shared by users. The study demonstrates, therefore, that even from a young age, users of social media acquire both curatorial skills and the ability to respond and react to the changes and problems they may encounter.

Celebrity curators

The role of celebrities as self-selecting tastemakers and cultural inter-mediaries has been the subject of much debate, particularly in relation to tv book clubs. Studies of Oprah's book club in the US (Collins 2010; Fuller and Rehberg Sedo 2013) and Richard and Judy's book club in the UK (Squires 2007; Cousins and Ramone 2011) have explored the impact that these clubs have both on book sales and on prevailing views of the place of literature in contemporary culture. More recently, attention has shifted to celebrity social media clubs, for example Reese Witherspoon's Instagram book club, and Emma Watson's intersectional feminist book club Our Shared Shelf which started out on Goodreads but now has a large following on Instagram.

In a recent study of the Kim Kardashian West 'Book Klub', Marsden (2018) argues that it is important to consider these ventures as marketing and branding opportunities, rather than focusing purely on the impact they may have on growing readerships and communities. In her study, Marsden examines the reactions to the setting up of the Klub in the press and on social media, and links them to the 'historical degradation of women's reading' (Driscoll 2014: 47), contrasting the response to Kardashian West with that to the more 'bookish' celebrity Emma Watson. Marsden locates her discussion of the Klub in the context of Kardashian West's career and attempt to rebrand herself after her retreat from social media in the aftermath of an attack in a Paris hotel. Although the article mainly focuses on the negative reactions to the Klub and the cultural snobbery of those who attacked its founder, it does go on to acknowl-edge the positive impact it had in terms of enthusing followers about books and reading.

Social media has long been recognised for its ability to create 'micro-celebrities' (Marwick 2013) or influencers who act as cultural inter-mediaries for their followers. In the UK, Zoe Sugg or 'Zoella' has become one of the most well-known of these influencers. She started out as a fashion vlogger but subsequently launched a career as a writer (author of the Girl Online trilogy) and host of the Zoella Book Club (later known as the Zoella & Friends Book Club), run in association with retailer WH Smith. As well as hosting Twitter takeovers and having its own hashtag (#zoellabookclub), the Club provides a space for followers to share their reading related images. In their study of the Zoella Book Club, Marsden and Branagh-Miscampbell (2019) trace the iconography of Zoella and her followers to images of young women reading from classical artwork, noting that the preference is still for domestic settings, and an aura of 'cosy femininity'. The article also engages with the reception the Book Club has received in the press, linking this as with Kim Kardashian West to the historical denigration of women's reading tastes and habits. However, the article does little to dispel the notion that the Club is a cosy haven for its readers, with the choice of reading material (Young Adult Fiction) and the aesthetic of the imagery selected for promoting the Club all connoting comfort and safe seclusion or withdrawal from the 'real world'.

Like the celebrity influencers who often promote or endorse books alongside other products, book subscription services such as Reading in Heels (rebranded in 2019 as www.reposed.co) offer a service packaging books as part of an 'amazing box of goodies'. Reading in Heels also offers the opportunity for subscribers to meet with like-minded readers in a members only digital book club if they want to go on to discuss books they have loved or 'felt a little meh about'. The target audience is clearly once again younger women, and readers for whom considering books as products to be consumed alongside chocolate, beauty products and other luxury goods seems second nature.

Literature on display

Walter Benjamin's (1999[1955]) essay about the joys of collecting books singled out the sense of anticipation and passion that the collector feels experiencing 'the most intimate relationship that one can have to objects'. He also turned on its head the idea of the relationship between passive objects and active collector: 'Not that they come alive in him; it is he who lives in them' (67). In this section I will demonstrate how social media's return to the 'aesthetic of bookishness' (Pressman 2014) can be seen as a response to the seeming dematerialisation of reading on digital devices, as well as a means for users to assert their readerly identities and to engage and play with books and book-related objects.

As well as book collecting, book history can also point to a long tradition of books used as objects for display. For example, Flint (2011) has shown how books were used in early photography to connote knowledge and intellectual capital. Meanwhile, Colclough (2011) has focused on how amongst the middle and upper classes books were put on display in drawing rooms as conversation pieces. Norrick-Rühl (2016) credits Thomas Masson as having coined the term 'domestic bookaflage' in 1923 to account for the practice of foregrounding highbrow books on one's bookshelf to impress guests. She links this practice to what she terms 'social media bookaflage' (6), where books adorn social media posts apparently at random, attributing this in part at least to the fact that ereaders have made it more difficult for readers to display to others what is being read.

Book collecting and the obsession with display can also be linked to more extreme behaviours. In Japan, the term Tsundoku refers to a person who owns vast quantities of unread reading material. It can be traced back to the late nineteenth century (Gerken 2018) as can the term bibliomania, an obsession with books that can lead to socially dis-preferred behaviours like hoarding but which can also be used to refer less pejoratively to people who are 'mad' about books. More recently, Batard's *How to Talk About Books You Haven't Read* (2007) provides a humorous account of the lengths people go to inserting bookish references into their conversations to gain prestige, impress others or talk about themselves.

Using photographs or other visual material to share one's reading also predates social media. From 2005 to 2010, novelist Jasper Fforde promoted the Thursday Nextreme Competition on his website, encouraging readers to post photographs of themselves reading his books in 'extreme' situations (http://www.jasperfforde.com/extreme/2010_entrants/leigh_20.html). Readers posted the images along with an accompanying explanatory narrative, producing a forerunner to the kinds of images displayed by @booksinsitu on Instagram, but also displaying the affinity of readers to the Fforde fandom.

Nevertheless, despite these precursors, the book as an object of display and even fetishisation can be found everywhere on social media. For example, the hashtag #book porn is used widely so that users can revel in their passion for books as an excessive or even transgressive act. However, it is perhaps the phenomenon of the **bookstagram**, the photographic equivalent of a still life in which the book has pride of place, that demonstrates how curation on social media can be a creative activity relying on considerable craft and artistry. Figure 4.1, which was created as part of a bookstagramming workshop I ran at Bournemouth University in 2018, demonstrates the basic principle of the form. However, in this case rather than the more usual book cover we have an extract from Joseph O'Connor's *Ghost Light* on an iPad (in dark mode), because the elderly participant (whose glasses also feature) can no longer read print books because of a degenerative eye condition. When the images are uploaded to Instagram, the poster will use hashtags to tag the content, and users who

Figure 4.1 Example of a bookstagram

find the image will often leave comments, sometimes opening up discussion about the book in question, but also remarking on the imagery and objects chosen and the design of the piece.

As well as readers, some authors participate in the activity. For example, novelist Andrea Dunlop (@andreadunlop) has over 1,000 posts and a profile which celebrates her love of the bookstagram (#Bookstagram all day), while author and comedian Samantha Irby (@bitchesgottaeat), regularly posts both bookstagrams and foodstagrams (pictures of dishes and meals). In an article for the *Huffington Post* (White 2017), Carly Watters, an American literary agent, talks about how she uses the platform to promote her clients, announce book deals and keep colleagues in the industry informed about what she is working on. In addition, the article features a marketing professional from the industry who talks of the importance of tailoring marketing to the particular platform, and of the importance of creating images that appear authentic and personalised rather than ones that appear photoshopped.

According to research conducted by McGowan Transcriptions (https://www.mcgowantranscriptions.co.uk/most-instagrammed-writers/) the most 'instagrammed' writer based on hashtag activity is Shakespeare, followed by Tolkien and Edgar Allan Poe. This repeats a pattern familiar from other digital rankings and polls, for example on the Kindle, where canonical authors or authors who feature on school curricula or have a high profile from film or tv adaptations feature prominently. McGowan also examined the most instagrammed works by author (*Romeo and Juliet*) and noted peaks in activity (around the dates of Shakespeare's birth and death, or the appearance of tv or film adaptations). The study is therefore useful not just for noting trends on social media, but for demonstrating how the impact of works of literature is intimately connected to current affairs, as well as being shaped by powerful social institutions.

While it would be all too easy to dismiss activities such as the bookstagram as turning the book into little more than an 'accessory', according to book designer Rachel Willey (cited by Connolly 2018), it also importantly provides a way for readers to share and display their reading material beyond the confines of the home, and highlights that the aesthetics of book covers is not just a matter for publishers and marketers, but for readers too. Indeed, Connolly's article goes so far as to suggest that the success of bookstagramming as a marketing technique is having an impact on book cover design.

One of the obvious attractions of Instagram for book lovers is that the images can be enjoyed regardless of language, and while posts tagged with #bookporn or #bookstagram are predominantly in English, the communities engaging in the activities are clearly multilingual. Nevertheless, despite the focus on the visual, Gallucci (2018) points to the importance of captions even on the most elaborate of bookstagrams for prompting discussion and debate. She further argues that 'book accounts exist to show off current reads and new releases, inspire people to renew their library cards or support their local bookstores, and step outside their literary comfort zones'. For the bookstagrammers interviewed by Gallucci, they clearly see it as their mission to help re-engage younger people with 'old-fashioned' books. However, it is dangerous to assume that older readers are excluded from these activities or to make blanket assumptions about young people's preferences, with research in fact pointing to the attractions of the 'retro' aesthetic of hardback books for younger readers (Thomas and Round 2012).

Book hauls, book porn and bookstagramming can of course be easily co-opted for commercial purposes, not just by individual authors but by publishers. Meanwhile, the potential negative impacts of displaying the self on social media have also been well documented (e.g. Marwick 2013). For the more adventurous, 'deep bookstagram' (Dockray 2019) brings together accounts dedicated to 'awkward, nostalgic book covers' (@vintage_covers), another featuring the strangest books dedicated to libraries (@awfullibrarybooks) and yet more bizarre, an account solely dedicated to images of various forms of ice cream with or near books (@ice_cream_books). Although not necessarily any more 'deep' than regular bookstagrams, what these accounts do point to is a willingness by users to satirise and parody the phenomenon, knowingly playing with its emerging tropes and conventions, while at the same time continuing to celebrate and revel in imagery associated with books and reading.

In an article for *The Guardian* on bookstgramming, Connolly (2018) argues that one of the reasons for its popularity is that the book serves to imply intellect on the part of the person creating the post. This can be linked to the wider phenomenon of 'virtue signalling', a term often attributed to Bartholomew (2015), who used it in an article for *The Spectator* to refer disparagingly to the act of saying the 'right' thing on social media so as to be seen to be kind and decent. Although the term has attracted criticism for its blanket ridiculing of predominantly liberal causes, it does capture the ways in which viral movements or 'clicktivism' can give users of social media the impression that they are not only following a cause but actively promoting it via social media. For Bartholomew, this is mere empty posturing, a weak substitute for acts of kindness or decency that might actually make a difference. In relation to books and reading, this plays out in the sense of books or reading being associated with moral superiority, not just in the sense of improving the person who owns the book or reads it, but in the broader sense of the very idea of book ownership and book reading as being worthy of note and affirmation from others. For example, BookRiot, a blog covering book-related news and reviews, regularly shares through its diverse social media accounts (on Pinterest, Twitter, Instagram, YouTube and Tumblr) slogans and motivational phrases celebrating books and reading ('Why can't I get paid to read all day?') alongside aspirational images of homes and reading spaces bedecked with books, or book-related objects, for example a whole series of images of cat bookends.

In her study of how readers use Pinterest to catalogue, curate and promote bookish behaviour, Rodger (2019) draws on New Materialism (discussed in the Introduction) and its challenge to the idea of material objects as passive. In particular, she explores how the activities of bookish 'pinners' draws on senses other than the visual (notably smell) to convey that books and reading are very much part of their everyday physical, bodily experiences, including the 'carnal'. Contrasting Pinterest with Instagram, Rodger argues that the former is more future focused and based on pinning one's desires, as opposed to Instagram and its concern with recording aspects of one's daily life. Nevertheless, Rodger is sensitive to the ways in which the activities of primarily female curation and sense-making on Pinterest are not only subject to commercial exploitation, but may provide a less than balanced representation of bookish sentiment because of the protections this particular platform places around its use of algorithms and data about users.

Tracking and cataloguing the literary

Book recommendation and online cataloguing sites such as Goodreads and LibraryThing allow users to quantify their reading and arrange their virtual books in a social context, reflecting the emergence of a 'recommendation culture' closely associated with the Web and with social media more specifically (van Dijck and Poell, 2013). According to Nakamura (2013: 4) they 'remediate earlier reading cultures where books were displayed in the home as signs of taste and status'. While there is clearly an element of functionality here, helping oneself and others to organise, prioritise and divide up one's reading into categories, there persists a sense in which users want to impress others in terms of the nature and sheer mass of reading they put on display, and in terms of their ability to curate that material. This sense of rivalry and competition between readers is reflective of a wider process of 'gamifying the reading experience' (Ray Murray and Squires 2013: 14), where direct comparison and the need to outdo others is always at least implicit.

In July 2019, an informal Twitter survey of authors by book marketing expert Sam Missingham (@samatlounge) uncovered strong distrust of the 'gang rule' of Goodreads, though many of those responding acknowledged they had very different experiences as readers. So while the site was seen by respondents as a good way to keep track of one's reading, as authors they were far less enthusiastic about how data about them was being used. Concerns have been raised (Striphas 2010; Nakamura 2013) about the ways in which the data generated by such sites can be mined and exploited for commercial purposes, as well as potentially being distributed or sold on to third parties. Thus even while she acclaims Goodreads as a 'utopia for readers', Nakamura reminds us that 'we are both collecting and being collected under a new regime of controlled consumerism' (2013: 6). She also raises concerns about the fact that such sites turn readers into workers and make user rights subject to constant change and attenuation. However, Driscoll and Rehberg Sedo (2019) use feminist standpoint theory to examine how Goodreads can give expression to intimate reading experiences and facilitates the sharing of emotional reactions to books. Combining content and sentiment analysis of nearly 700 reviews, they argue that the site constitutes a new cultural phenomenon and a unique resource for researchers of reading and readers.

Literary data

The risks attaching to social media usage have been brought into the foreground through high profile stories about data surveillance and abuses of data discussed in the Introduction. These have reignited debates about the ethics of activities such as data mining, and raised awareness of the ways in which seemingly innocuous everyday acts on social media are the object of constant surveillance and scrutiny. As a consequence, many of the previously freely available tools for extracting data from social media have disappeared or been monetised. Nevertheless, at the time of writing, it is still possible to access **analytics** via platforms such as Twitter simply by visiting your user profile on the website. So for example, I can see at a glance who is 'engaging' with my tweets on a map of the world, see a breakdown of my audience in terms of gender, and get advice on how to grow my audience. As well as providing data for individual authors, these tools can also provide useful statistical analysis for all kinds of literary organisations and events. In addition, they can provide information on how readers and audiences engage with literary texts, for example by tracking data on activities such as group reads (discussed in Chapter 6).

The field of the digital humanities has responded to this data revolution by reimagining the ways in which we might engage with the literary, for example examining the 'distant' and large-scale alongside 'close' reading, or making use of tools that give us unprecedented access to 'real' readers (Thomas and Round 2012). Of course, the idea of treating literature as a large body of work which can be curated and analysed systematically has a much longer history in corpus linguistics. Nevertheless, quantified approaches are still met with suspicion and can be very labour intensive (Hammond 2016). A major criticism is often that this labour may in fact produce very little in terms of new insights. However, the true value of such approaches is that they can reveal hidden patterns in texts we feel we may know very well, or produce unexpected, serendipitous results because they are not confined to the assumptions or expectations of the individual researcher and his or her interpretation of what that text may mean.

In his analysis of Amazon reviews, Finn (2012) employed network visualisation and text mining to examine purchasing patterns but also to allow him to compare the structures of prestige and canonicity across both consumer reviews and those offered by professional critics. He did so in relation to a specific text, Toni Morrison's *Beloved*, and found that the consumer reviews provided a diversity of approaches in comparison to the dominant 'geometries of prestige' (189) of the professional reviews. The use of digital tools allowed him to zoom in on specific usages, particularly how the word 'black' was understood as a literary concept across the two corpora, and how the consumer reviews made explicit argument and anxieties about the issues raised by Morrison's text that were unlikely to be found in the professional reviews.

In his comparative study of professional and Amazon customer reviews of Kiran Desai's *The Inheritance of Loss*, Daniel Allington (2016) turns to thematic coding and social network analysis to identify patterns across over 100 reviews. In particular, presenting findings in the form of social network graphs helped him establish how the professional reviews tended towards homogenisation, while the Amazon reviews reflected a popular aesthetic sensibility. The analysis also provided more detailed insights, for example that the professional reviews focus on humour, while the customer reviews tend to dwell on criticism of characters.

Sentiment analysis has been used by Driscoll (2015) to study the emotions surrounding the 2013 Melbourne Writers Festival across over 20,000 tweets and 900 survey responses. Driscoll claims that this allowed her to develop a new approach to studying audience engagement and the various ways in which festivals facilitate shared intimacies between writers and readers. Like Allington, Driscoll combined the study of larger data sets with qualitative close reading, arguing that sentiment analysis can be used as the basis for targeted close readings because of the high-level insights into emotional language that it provides. This means that reflection on the methods used, as well as the ethical implications of using large scale data sets of this kind features as a main focus of such studies, rather than being something that is either taken for granted or relegated to a short and tokenistic subsection.

Julian Pinder's (2012) study of Library Thing, an online cataloguing site for book lovers does not so much draw on the digital humanities toolkit as provide a close analysis of the kinds of affinity facilitated by the site's algorithmic links. Pinder is interested in the ways in which the site allows for the display of a kind of 'performative consumption' which carries with it the intellectual, aesthetic and moral values he argues are imputed specifically to books and to literature. Thus he sees Library Thing not so much as usurping as working alongside other institutions which support and promote literary and reading cultures. He further-more recognises that the site is distinctive in offering users the ability to identify and participate in multiple groups or interpretive communities simultaneously, as well as to link to groups outside the site, through connecting users with their profiles on Facebook or Twitter. For Pinder, Library Thing is an illustration of the kind of knowledge work that digital humanities scholars argue is so intrinsic to the internet, providing users with the possibility of identifying and understanding how that knowledge is held and shared. Although Pinder acknowledges the limita-tions of his study, and points to ethnographic analysis as being able to provide the evidence of meaningful connections between users that his methods cannot, he is able to link his discussion and analysis of the site's technical infrastructure to provide telling observations of the ways in which affinity is generated and consolidated between users as a natural function of the way in which information of all kinds is organised and managed.

As well as allowing for new ways of approaching the analysis of large data sets, fully engaging with the digital in these ways means revisiting the myth of the sole author and re-engaging with the social nature of text (Bath et al. 2018). In this respect, work from the digital humanities inter-sects with book history and its emphasis on books as emerging from a complex communications circuit made even more complex in the digital age (Ray Murray and Squires 2013). An emphasis on books as part of a social-material complex also has a long tradition in book history. But work from the digital humanities further foregrounds the myriad ways texts are mal-leable, facilitates engagement with texts that might previously only have been accessible wearing white gloves in locked rooms in libraries, and allows citizen archivists, curators and editors to participate in the activity of preserving and disseminating hidden or forgotten works (Bath et al. 2018).

Much of the excitement generated by digital humanities methods and approaches responds to the sheer quantities of data that now seem so freely available, whether that is data from digitised text, or data in the form of user input. It is the latter that is of particular interest to scholars interested in reception, as online forums and social media appear to provide us with access to endless data about the habits, tastes and preferences of readers and audiences. However, a key limitation is that the analysis is confined to the visible and observable, so the unspoken ways in which people might react, follow, or contribute cannot be captured. For example, in online communities, lurkers may make up a considerable percentage of overall users but as the term suggests, their presence tends to be seen as negative, with few studies to date actually taking the time to try to understand what lurkers do, what motivates them, or how individuals might lurk on some sites while actively and visibly contributing to others.

The new tools available to digital humanities scholars therefore open up the activity of curation not just in terms of sheer scale, but also in terms of who can participate and engage with the collection, selection and dissemination of literary materials. Moreover, work from the digital humanities usefully foregrounds the role of interpretation and narrativisation in relation to how data is made meaningful, drawing on skills and approaches from traditional humanities subjects. This kind of tethering can helpfully highlight how data is animated by different groups in different ways (Dourish and Cruz 2018). And importantly, in the era of fake news it reminds us that data is not self-evident and incontestable, foregrounding how narrativisation imposes sequence and causality as well as bringing order and meaning.

A certain degree of scepticism is healthy when it comes to assessing the data provided by sites such as Amazon and GoodReads even though they may appear entirely automated and thus not subject to user error or bias. For example, it is not difficult to see how 'most popular' ratings can be skewed by users voting more than once and it is easy to find books both being miscategorised and appearing in multiple categories. Access to such data can also be subject to change: while Amazon still makes available information about 'trending titles' and 'top new releases', it has removed the facility for Kindle users to access 'Popular Highlights', instead providing access only to the user's own notes and highlights. Simon Rowberry's (2016) work on the traces readers leave on their e-readers relied on the public facing website for collecting data, and amongst his preliminary findings were some clear patterns emerging in terms of the books highlighted (Young Adult fiction and classics, self-help books) as well as the individual passages selected (YA readers tended to highlight 'spoilers').

Scholars from the digital humanities and book history including Rowberry (2015) and Kirschenbaum (2016) are turning to the emerging fields of media archaeology and internet and web history to better understand the impact that large scale but also seemingly insignificant technological changes can have on both the production and consumption of literary texts. They provide invaluable and detailed records and analysis of software and hardware upgrades that otherwise would be easily lost or forgotten, as well as histories of browsers and web domains. Meanwhile, platform studies, and platform biographies of the kind being developed by internet scholars such as Baym et al. (2016), employ user interviews, archival materials and platform data to chart the changes and significant landmarks and controversies relating to specific platforms over time. Such work demonstrates how scholars are adapting to the rapid pace of change that characterises the digital, including social media. In so doing they are contributing to a greater understanding of the importance and significance of the need for preserving and charting not just technological artefacts, interfaces and software redesigns and upgrades, but also user experiences, and their place and role in social and cultural life.

This chapter has explored the often unseen and unrecognised work that helps to disseminate, promote and preserve literary and cultural activity on social media. That work can be conducted by a whole range of people and for a whole range of motivations from the commercial to the fannish. As with the renewed interest and focus on the paratextual in studies of contemporary culture (discussed in the Introduction), this shift in emphasis beyond the confines of the individual text or work, and beyond the kinds of hierarchies that divide and often devalue different kinds of contribution, hopefully brings a renewed sense of the idea of literature as something that is collectively achieved or achievable, and as something that can be shaped and shared by many people in many different ways.

5 Literary movements in the network era

The world wide web and social media provide a means for people to discover and connect with others that share their interests on a scale and with the kind of ease not previously possible. These groupings are often ephemeral but they can offer a more stable and fixed space for people to return to, leading to the formation of lasting relationships and creating a strong sense of identity and place. Facebook groups are a popular way for fans, writers, artists and readers to share content and interact with each other. Groups can decide not only who gets to join, but what rights of access (if any) others may have to view or share in discussions. For example @myhaikupond (discussed in Chapter 3) has a bespoke 'Academy' on Facebook which acts as a co-writing space or workshop for participants but in the 'safe space' of a closed group managed by two administrators.

Concerned about privacy and toxicity, many users seek out services that offer further protections, such as the messenger service WhatsApp (owned by Facebook) which offers end-to-end encryption so that only the sender and receiver can access content. Thus, while social media is often associated with openness and connection, users may choose to set limits and boundaries to restrict access to others, or to promote and deepen the sense of belonging and intimacy that they may seek from membership of a group.

This chapter will begin with a critical reflection on the concepts of community and network/networking used throughout the preceding discussion. Previous chapters have explored how readers form networks and communities across social media, and how authors can cultivate followers and create a strong sense of a group identity for some of their readers. However, the main focus of this chapter will be on how we move from loose affinities and ephemeral connections between individuals and groups to the formation of groupings that either self-identify as literary movements, or that are treated as such by cultural commentators and literary critics.

The problem with 'community'

The term 'community' is used ubiquitously but not without controversy or critique to refer to all kinds of social formations online and across social media. From Anderson's (1983) notion of 'imagined' communities, to the work of Rheingold (2000[1993]) on the 'virtual' community, the idea that digital spaces can provide alternatives to, or new kinds of, community particularly for those who may feel marginalised or disempowered has widespread traction and appeal. The term also allows for the sense that groups of people who come together in spaces mediated by the digital often go on to develop strong affective bonds (Thomas 2011b; Thomas and Round 2016) or to build on common interests and concerns to activate for change. Nevertheless, the blanket use of the term risks denuding it of its source meaning, in particular the notion that community and communality are rooted in social and economic conditions that shape who members are and what they can do, but that they in turn can act on to change and improve. As a result, the term community can easily be hijacked by corporations and marketers as a way to encourage loyalty and monetise attention (Davies 2017). Other objections to the term are based on the fact that the ephemeral and often asymmetrical relationships that form in online communities bear no resemblance to the idea of community as something rooted in time and place that provides a sense of stability and belonging to members.

Gee's notion of 'affinity spaces' (2004) is a response to some of these misgivings, and speaks to the geographically distributed, technologically mediated and fluidly populated social groupings familiar from fan cultures and other online spaces where people associate and feel a sense of belonging, but which remain open so that anyone can come and go at will. The concept of affinity spaces covers a wide spectrum of forms of participation, from casual lurking to helping set up and manage the space. In addition, it allows for variation in the extent to which the spaces may be nurturing and welcoming, or adversarial and competitive. Nevertheless, the language associated with Gee's affinity spaces is still couched in some sense of 'us' and of the 'common' and the 'shared'. It also speaks of choice and agency – 'everyone can, if they wish, produce and not just consume' (Gee and Hayes 2012: 137) – and of a general atmosphere of 'encouragement' and 'facilitation'.

More specifically focused on social media, Zappavigna's concept of 'ambient affiliation' (2011) addresses how hashtags can foster and actively build a sense of community amongst users who may never meet or even interact directly with one another. This results from the fact that, according to Zappavigna, when people search online they are looking not just for information or content, but for communities based on shared values. Equally, while posts on social media may not require or expect a response, Zappavigna argues that they nonetheless display a 'social need among users to engage with other voices' (790) while devices such as the hashtag presuppose 'a virtual community of interested listeners' (791). For Zappavigna, one of the distinguishing features of interpersonal communication on Twitter is the fact that the affiliation with others is about what 'interest(s) you in the given moment' (804) but she argues for methods that locate 'what is being negotiated with language within particular patterns of social processes' (804) rather than merely noting connections as social network analysis might do. Specifically drawing on the features and affordances of social media, Zappavigna's work is important in demonstrating how affiliation is negotiated by users, rather than being something that can just be asserted or assumed. Moreover, the concept of ambience allows for the idea that affiliation on social media may be ephemeral and fleeting but is 'always on' for users engaged in the constant process of seeking and sifting.

The concept of virality takes us more deeply into the territory of the random and the diffuse, allowing for the ways in which actors on social media can behave selfishly and so as to undermine and disrupt rather than nurture or build. In both fan studies and studies of internet culture more broadly, the term 'toxicity' (discussed in the Introduction) is widely used to refer to displays of cruelty, abuse and general nastiness on social media, as well as how such displays so easily escalate and spread.

Net-working

In many contexts, the terms social networking and social media are used interchangeably. The term network is widely used as a verb, particularly in the sense of seeking out and cultivating those whom you would like to be associated with and linked to, often in the context of professional life. The latter sense can carry negative connotations, implying something that has to be cultivated or worked at, as opposed to connections and affinities that might develop more organically or naturally. Social networking draws on the idea of the network from computing, where data is exchanged, resources are shared to ease the flow of information and communication. Social network analysis (discussed in Chapter 4) examines the relations between actors in a network in terms of nodes and links (or ties) and visualises and concretises these linkages into graphs and maps. As well as being used for the study of online networks and communities, SNA has also been used to uncover lesser known historical networks and how they may have influenced the political and cultural life of the day. Meanwhile, Actor Network Theory (ANT), 'seeks to explain social order not through an essentialized notion of "the social" but through the networks of connections among human agents, technologies, and objects' (Couldry 2008: 93). While it could be argued that a clear distinction needs to be maintained between the idea of the network, linking and connecting individuals, and a community based on shared interests, in practice many spaces can in fact be both. For example, Davies (2017) argues that Wattpad is both a community and a network, a way for people to share interests but also to build networks through linking individual user profiles.

Rainie and Wellman (2012) see the kind of networking that the internet and social media has facilitated as providing a whole new 'social operating system' connecting 'networked individuals' who 'actively maneuver' (18) amongst looser, more fragmented networks rather than sitting embedded in tight and hierarchical social groups as in the past. In their understanding of the network, not all members need know one another, but they need to be able to find ways to work together and remember who performs which role, relying on trust as their primary currency. In Rainie and Wellman's conception, therefore, individuals need to rely on their own resourcefulness as well as the support of others, and to acknowledge that although connections may be thin the different social order that has emerged 'gives people new ways to solve problems and meet social needs' (9).

Literary movements

Applied to the field of literature, the concept of the network further undermines the myth of the author as a romantic, isolated genius. Similarly, the kind of networking technology makes possible has implications for how we understand the traditional notion of the literary movement, particularly where this relies on maintaining an absolute divide between literature and popular culture, the remoteness of authors from their audiences, and the need to build boundaries around writers and their texts for the purposes of definition and classification. This is especially true of literary movements associated with experimentalism and the avant garde, such as the early twentieth century Modernist movement, subject to constant accusations of elitism, and to frequent attempts at reappraisal (e.g. Bergonzi 1986; Bucur 2017).

Like literary genres, the criteria by which literary movements are defined are constantly shifting and contested. For example, national boundaries (e.g. English Romanticism) may be problematic, as may attempts to define movements in terms of periods and even dates (when did Romanticism begin and end exactly?). Literary movements may helpfully, but occasionally problematically group artists and writers together purely in terms of their gender, ethnicity or sexuality. Formal characteristics of the literary text, a defined style, or frequency of certain stylistic features, for example fictional dialogue (Thomas 2012), may lead writers to be grouped together who might not otherwise be seen as close contemporaries or as sharing any kind of world view. Like genre, too, despite the contestability of these definitions and categories, the idea of the movement remains seductive and provides useful and functional ways for readers and critics to search out connections and correspondences and to curate the potentially vast field of literature for often highly practical purposes, e.g. teaching literature, arranging books on bookshelves or in a bookstore.

Perhaps it is inevitable that writers and artists who set out to challenge norms and to pursue the experimental seek support from each other and from the sense that they are participating in a wider movement. Rather than the word 'movement', the term 'collective' may be preferred if the group of writers and artists perceive themselves to be operating on the margins of the mainstream, or in opposition to dominant ideologies or aesthetic practices. The term collective can therefore suggest a grouping that is looser or more democratic, where the organisation of the group and decisions about its identity are taken collectively and on an ongoing basis.

Thus, while the internet and social media may facilitate the publishing of new works and finding new audiences, it could be said that they also amplify the reliance on networks to support artists and to bring their works to prominence. In particular, the idea that the contemporary media landscape is more about narrowcasting to niche audiences (Jenkins 2006a; Mittell 2015) than broadcasting to the masses, highlights how audiences' shared tastes and preferences can be catered to (but also shaped) in ways not previously possible. Examples of this would be tv channels dedicated to specific genres (science fiction; crime; cookery) suggesting that you can find your 'tribe' by using the search and linking facilities that new platforms help make available.

Instapoetry

Online and on social media, commonality or a sense of affinity may be established primarily on the basis of a shared method, style, but may just as easily be about the fact that the activity takes place on the same platform. Chapter 3 focused primarily on a range of examples of what I called 'Twitterliterature' and how writers and artists have responded to the affordances of the platform, more specifically the seeming restrictions of being confined to 140/280 characters. Some examples were provided of experimentation around performance and the poetic. However, it is Instagram and YouTube that are most closely associated with emerging poetic voices, specifically the so-called 'Instapoets' who have established a distinctive presence on that platform, but who also almost always perform and present their work across multiple platforms. In an article on the 'rock stars of poetry', the BBC reported that the hashtag #poetry is said to have attracted more than 27 million posts on Instagram in 2018 (Freeman-Powell 2019). At around the same time as the BBC article appeared, *The Guardian* published two articles by Ferguson on Insta-poetry, one detailing how the phenomenon had boosted the sales of poetry among 'political millennials' (2019a) and the other focusing on how young female poets writing online are attracting a diverse audience (Ferguson 2019b). Ferguson argued that the poetry appearing on Insta-gram was appealing to 'millennials' because it cut through the verbiage of contemporary political discourse and addressed their hunger for nuance. Moreover, she links Instapoetry to the #metoo movement speaking out against sexual harassment and exploitation, and sees in the new voices of the female Instapoets an outlet for the expression of the female sexual gaze.

In October 2018 an edition of BBC Radio 4's *The Verb*, hosted by Ian McMillan (whose own social media presence is discussed in Chapter 6), was dedicated to Instapoetry, and featured Instapoets Yrsa Daley-Ward and Johnathan Rice. McMillan drew many parallels between his use of Twitter, which he likened to a live performance, and Instapoetry, describing his fondness for a 'caffeine hit of language' and comparing the writing found on these platforms to the tradition of the commonplace book. In relation to Johnathan Rice's work, the show drew comparisons with traditional, print-based haikus. Meanwhile Yrsa Daley-Ward spoke of her work as being compressed, like epiphanies, providing a pleasur-able 'intense shock' and a space between the short poems which allows the reader to pause for breath. While the focus of the discussion was predominantly on language and form, it did touch on the visual aspects of poetry and the ways in which Instapoetry relies on image and elicits visual responses such as emojis from followers. The fact that a whole edition of the programme was given over to this subject, and that the poets featured were only discussed in relation to their work on Instagram, helped to consolidate the idea of a distinctive poetic move-ment evolving while also identifying connections with poetic tradition and with other forms of literary play on social media.

Perhaps the idea of the movement has always had more traction for poets than prose fiction writers. This may be because of the close asso-ciation between poetry and public spaces, and the practical need to group together to ensure a decent audience. However, it may equally be because of the fact that since the late twentieth century (at least in the Anglophone world) poetry has been perceived as a more niche activity, nearly always less lucrative as a profession than novel writing, and with fewer poets gaining the kind of celebrity accorded to writers of fiction.

Poetry works well on social media because it can be integrated with both audio and visual material, and because it can just as easily provide short and rapid responses to current affairs as deeply personal and intimate shared experiences. Many of the Instapoets (most of whom are of the generation who have grown up with mobile and social media) deal with mental health and body image issues. For example Charly Cox's (2018) collection of poetry *she must be mad*, published in print form after she rose to prominence as a writer on Instagram, deals with her depression, anxiety, as well as other millennial 'coming-of-age' experiences such as using dating apps and following celebrity social media accounts. In addition to her Instagram account, Cox has used YouTube to create short video poems (one for every day in May 2016). As discussed in Chapter 3, what social media literature brings in this context is the opportunity to 'follow' the poet as she attempts to work through her issues. As the epigraph for *she must be mad* tells us, what makes Cox's collection distinctive is the fact that it is 'written by someone who's still in the thick of it', not a success story telling others how to overcome their problems, but someone who can create 'relatable' (Thompson 2018) content for the generation for whom and to whom she primarily speaks.

Another example of this relatability is the fact that the collection features handwritten poems and a photograph of the poet with her grandad. In this respect, the collection retains a close link with the aesthetic of Instagram, or Pinterest, making art from what is to hand, or creating thematic collages from multiple media. The language also makes specific reference to social media practices, for example in the poem 'filters' which makes explicit reference to Instagram and Photoshopping.

One of the poets most closely identified with Instagram is Rupi Kaur because of her extensive use of her own photography ('her tool to tell the world how she envisions it' (https://rupikaur.com/photography/)). Although she has published print anthologies of her work and tours regularly, her Instagram account has a huge following (over 3.8 million as of November 2019), combining poetry with hand drawn illustrations, and interspersing poetry with portrait shots of Rupi on her own or on her travels. It is all too easy to dismiss this as the celebrification of the poet, or as writing that relies on flashy visual triggers rather than inviting close scrutiny or prolonged engagement with the rhythms and words of the published pieces. Indeed, Instapoets, especially female poets such as Rupi Kaur, Charly Cox and Lang

Leav, are frequently attacked for writing self-indulgent pieces, or for wallowing in their own misery.

Of course, there is a very long history in literature of would-be female writers being attacked or disparaged for being overly personal or emotional. Although the Instapoets' collections outsell those of most other contemporary poets, few have been subjected to critical analysis beyond reviews in newspapers or magazines. The target audience for much of this writing is other women: on the back cover of the print publication of Cox's *she must be mad* the words woman and girl are used repeatedly and the endorsement comes from Pandora Sykes, a journalist and podcaster known mainly for her work on fashion and travel, but who is, also like Cox, a campaigner for mental health. Likewise, the subjects of many of the poems in the collection are given the pronouns 'she' and 'her' and 'boys' or 'he' are the main objects of attention, or the antagonists in the female subjects' attempts to overcome their feelings of worthlessness. While of course this does not preclude the possibility that the readership for the poems may be much broader, it does perhaps explain why some critics feel the work of Cox and others can so easily be dismissed.

In early 2018, poet Rebecca Watts published an article in *PN Review* attacking the rise of poetry based on honesty, accessibility and instant gratification and lacking any knowledge of versification or poetic tradition, taking aim at Rupi Kaur and spoken word poet Hollie McNish whose latest collection she had been asked to review. The article pulled no punches in describing McNish's work as 'garbled literal statements with the odd approximate rhyme thrown in', arguing that poetry as the 'loftiest of literary arts' was being targeted for 'invasion' by this new generation of 'amateurs'. In the article, Watts draws comparisons between the rise of this kind of poetry and the cult of the amateur with the populist politics of Donald Trump. Equating social media with a 'dumbing effect', Watts makes no reference to the fact that McNish and Kaur are primarily known as spoken word artists, nor does she show any interest in attempting to understand how they engage with their audiences and with the affordances of social media, but instead focuses purely on 'craft' in terms of their print outputs. Following the publication of the article, *The Guardian* (Flood and Cain 2018) reported on the split that it had caused in the poetry world, citing poets such as Lemn Sissay and Don Paterson who expressed support for those attacked by Watts, but leaving vague 'the many supportive responses' received by the editor of the journal, shared with the newspaper but not, sadly, with the rest of us.

In an article published on the digital media website *Mashable*, Byager (2018) provided a robust rebuttal to Watts, with support from Judith Palmer, Director of the Poetry Society, and Eleanor Spencer-Regan from

Durham University amongst others. Accusing denigrators of Instapoetry of 'mislabelling' the poetry by judging it against the standards and conventions of print, 'poetry native to Instagram' is instead celebrated for its diversity and for providing a similar 'gateway' for younger readers as the Harry Potter novels. Spencer-Regan likewise makes the point that the tone and vocabulary of this poetry is distinctive, reminiscent of the language of self-help and self-improvement that provides such an important outlet for young people struggling with issues of identity and self-worth. The article defends the poetry's claims to provide something 'relatable' and sincere on a platform that has become associated with inauthenticity and toxicity. While the article shies away from taking head on the criticisms of quality, instead it argues that Instapoetry should be seen as its own 'budding genre', and as addressing a younger audience than the one *PN Review* typically speaks to. In this sense, some of the arguments used to defend Instapoetry seem very reminiscent of those used in relation to fanfiction and debates about the extent to which it should be considered within the context of the literary (Thomas 2011b).

In addition to the phenomenon of Instapoetry, social media offers many opportunities for spoken word poets to broadcast their work to new audiences through links to videos of performances or specially commissioned pieces. In the UK Kate Tempest has used YouTube to share public performances of her work. She also has her own website, has published with established literary publishers (Bloomsbury, Picador), produced albums of her work and regularly puts on 'shows'. Likewise, Shane Koyczan's performances of his work are easily accessible via his website and through his Facebook page (@shanekoyczanpoetry) YouTube channel, Twitter and Instagram accounts, all of which attract large followings.

As well as issues of quality, Instapoetry and especially the use of YouTube raise questions of authorship, where collaborators may include video directors, actors and other artists and technicians who contribute to the production of the performances or short films fronted and scripted by the poets. Although the poets clearly do take ownership of the words, for example by publishing the pieces in print anthologies, there is a strong sense of a collaborative ethos, and of inviting engagement from the wider audience who can post responses or share their own experiences via comments.

Wu Ming

Alongside informal networks and communities of practice, and the rise of the celebrity poet, social media provides a space for groups to self-define according to a particular stance or ideology. Perhaps one of the most well-known examples is the Wu Ming 'band' or collective that first emerged from the arts scene in Bologna in 2000 and went on to publish fiction and non-fiction as well as making films. The blog and Facebook page of the 'band' also contributed to their notoriety, leading to the emergence of the Wu Ming Foundation, described as a grassroots federation of collectives that includes people inspired to take part in discussion around the group's ideas, as well as those creating their own artworks, or collaborating with others in labs and 'inquiry groups'. The focus on the group or collective and the playful use of names (the group was originally named after British black footballer Luther Blissett) demonstrates how resistance to convention, and especially the idea of the author, helps define the group's ethos.

The extent to which the engagement with social media has enhanced the collective's activities remains a matter of some debate. Thus while Patti (2016) follows the evolution of the group's experiments with collaborative authorship from print to social media, she argues both that the input of readers is limited and that the possibility of experimentation is restricted by the fact that collaborative narratives on social media need 'to comply with a predetermined narrative design' (55). Meanwhile, Vadde's (2017) discussion of the collective focuses on their publishing practices and alignment with the so-called gift economy to open up their work for circulation. Although she considers their work as informed by a 'Marxist-anarchist ethos' and an avant garde movement built on manifesto, activism and pranksterism, she also considers their work alongside that of other collectivities including fan cultures and online writing communities as part of a wider critique of institutional histories of literature and attempts to 'absorb audiences into their worlds' (48).

Alt Lit

Like Wu Ming, the Alt Lit movement that emerged around 2011 started publishing in online magazines and blogs and primarily consisted of male writers. Since the term Alt Lit was first coined, both the writers themselves and the cultural commentators who write about them have sought to identify shared concepts and practices. For example, Goldsmith has written that the Alt Lit 'writing community' 'harnesses the casual affect and jagged stylistics of social media as the basis of their works' (2014), producing a body of work 'marked by direct speech, expressions of aching desire, and wide-eyed sincerity'. Goldsmith goes on to further identify aspects of language and style defining the group, for example its 'emo-heavy, homespun language'. However, he also recognises that what defines this group as 'alt' is their embrace of 'abundant typos, and bad grammar', and that many subgroups have already emerged, such as 'weird Twitter' and 'flarf' (an early twenty-first century Internet poetry movement based on exploiting and repurposing the language of searches on the Web) such that any attempt at a static or fixed characterisation of the movement becomes problematic.

Goldsmith further attempts to locate Alt Lit writers in terms of where and when their works are found (anthologies and events) and by listing and naming recognisable 'authors'. In addition, he traces links with earlier literary works and movements (Imagism, the Beats), and explores the social context that has produced Alt Lit, specifically its links with feminism and environmental politics. Goldsmith's discussion of Alt Lit also takes place alongside his exploration of the concept of uncreative writing, where he attempts to account for how the seemingly mechanistic and robotic generation of language associated with the digital (discussed in Chapters 1, 2 and 3) can be harnessed by writers including those of the Alt Lit movement to re-examine and re-define how we understand creativity and the making and sharing of meaning. Included in Goldsmith's account of the 'uncreative' is the recycling, appropriation and even plagiarism of content, but also the possibility of a machinic audience for this new writing. For the young writers like those of the Alt Lit movement that Goldsmith engages with 'the act of writing is literally moving language from one place to another' (2011: 3) and they share a joyous revelling in 'the wonderful rhythm of repetition, the spectacle of the mundane' (4).

In his discussion of Alt Lit, Hammond describes them as being 'tied together by their extremely active use of the internet and social media' (2016: 142). He discusses their collective approach to publication, particularly how they embrace the freedoms of digital publishing, and their writing practices (working collaboratively and editing/updating based on ongoing feedback). He also talks of the movement in terms of shared techniques ('recontextualized quotation' 143) and content ('repurposed ephemera' 143) and describes the 'characteristic tone' of Alt Lit as 'flat, monotonous, and brutally undecorated' (143). For Hammond, therefore, the Alt Lit movement represents a challenge to the idea that originality and excitement should define the literary, and instead the focus is on 'mining vast quantities of digital text for unexpected or unapprehended beauty' (144).

The publication of *The Yolo Pages* in 2014 perhaps represents the apotheosis of the Alt Lit movement. It served both to anthologise the work of key artists, many of whose works might otherwise have been lost, and to provide (by way of its critical introduction) some insights into the movement's key aims. Bringing together work by some of the most high-profile Alt Lit writers, including Steve Roggenbuck, one of the anthology's editors, the book also features examples of flarf, weird Twitter, and highly visual content. Throughout the introduction 'alt lit' appears in quotation marks to highlight, we are told, its resistance to labelling. Yet at the same time the introduction is at pains to establish key shared values (an embrace of the internet, spirituality and a desire to change the world) and an intent to include diverse content such as network names that may come to be seen as 'the unseen literature of this generation' (@postcrunk, 148).

'This generation' is defined as those who have grown up with the internet, and the introduction makes great play of the fact that half of the contributors featured are under twenty five. Cory Stephens' coinage of the term 'alt lit' is held up as the inaugural moment for the movement, linking artists primarily concerned with an online 'scene' gathered together by Stephens on Tumblr with the community emerging from a culture of sharing and collaboration across social media platforms (primarily Facebook, Tumblr and Twitter). The shared aesthetic of the writers featured in the collection is described as 'visual, contemporary, and aggressively engaging' (Roggenbuck, Scott and Younghans 2014: 5) and the design of the book (with its visual pun on The Yellow Pages directory) is reminiscent of the zine and its community focus and diy ethos. Nevertheless, author bios are provided and individual writers such as Tao Lin are given prominence as a 'vital pillar' (107) of the movement.

While the Alt Lit writers relied heavily on social media to share and perform their work, their success and celebrity undoubtedly owed a great deal to their skills in self-promotion. Hammond attributes this to the fact that on social media 'the line between *talking about* and *writing* Alt Lit is so blurred' (2016: 144). He furthermore notes how Roggenbuck openly discussed his writing in the context of 'branding' and embodies the 'rapprochement of lifestyle marketing with literature' (145).

However, the celebrity of the Alt Lit writers has proved double-edged. In particular, the movement has been beset by controversy following accusations of sexual violence made against several of the leading figures including Tao Lin and Stephen Tully Dierks. Indeed, many of the writers and poets who first came to prominence with the movement have withdrawn completely from the internet and social media. For example, Steve Roggenbuck's website (www.steveroggenbuck.com) tells us he is focusing on 'school and activism' rather than producing new work, and mainly functions as an archive for his work. This means that the sense of 'active community' and improvisation that he describes as being so crucial to his poetry can now only be experienced at a distance.

As with the Instapoets discussed earlier, much of the impact of the Alt Lit movement came from the sense they created for their followers that they were witnessing the making of literature as something raw and in progress, and as something that they can contribute to, even if that means buying the merchandise sold in live performance. While some forms of Instapoetry and other artists' use of social media can be primarily about broadcasting work that could equally appear in print or another medium, Alt Lit writers such as Roggenbuck did see themselves as 'creating poetry IN the unique forms of each platform' (cited by Geffen n.d.) and they sought to showcase the performative potential of those platforms as sites for creative play and expression. In an online interview/performance of his work, Roggenbuck begins by saying he doesn't know if the videos he posts on YouTube should be called poetry or not, or whether they are 'what happens when a poet decides to start making YouTube videos' (https://www.youtube.com/watch?v=7BvfDa PgMzo) and extensively uses air quotes as though to signal to his audience his lack of pretension. Moreover, he portrays himself throughout as someone who is acting in opposition to the 'establishment' (despite acknowledging his debt to Walt Whitman) and speaks openly about how he cultivated his following and was initially excited by social media because of the reach and access to audiences they could provide.

As with Roggenbuck, most accounts of the work of Tao Lin sit on the fence when it comes to making judgements about literary merit or lasting contribution. Especially in the mainstream press, an alibi is often offered by reviewers who confess themselves bemused by the writing but convinced that the writers must be speaking for their generation. Interviews with both writers doubtless contribute to this uncertainty as the extent to which they are being serious is often in doubt. However, there is typically far less doubt about their immediate and short term impact. For example, Sansom (2013) refers to Tao Lin as 'one of the first writers to have been formed not through traditional page and print culture but in and through social media and the internet'.

Tao Lin first made his name as a poet but has subsequently focused more on prose with the publication of novels, short stories and nonfiction. With Mira Gonzalez, Tao Lin published *Selected Tweets* based on their Twitter accounts between 2008 and 2014 in an attempt, according to Gonzalez, to show 'there really isn't any difference in value between poetry and Twitter' (interviewed by Escoria 2015). However, in the same interview, Tao Lin goes on to compare the Tweets to short stories and describes the book based on their Tweets as an example of a fragmented linear narrative.

Taipei (2013) by Tao Lin plays to many of the themes associated with the Alt Lit movement as it follows its protagonist, Paul, a semi-autobiographical version of Tao Lin, from party to party, charting in increasing amount of detail the quantities of drugs taken by him and

Erin, the woman he randomly marries. Frederick Barthelme's blurb for *Taipei* hails its ability to convey the 'ultra self-conscious' way we live our lives today, and describes the novel as 'a paean to the minutely examined life'. The novel has also been linked to the post-postmodern, particularly in its depiction of contemporary consciousness as a kind of 'streaming', and in the narrative's constant sense of self-parody (McDougall 2019).

The novel name checks celebrity gossip websites Jezebel and dlisted as well as 4chan, a site which enjoys a certain notoriety for allowing anonymous often highly inflammatory posts and for helping to spread various internet memes. Indeed, Paul does not appear to devote much time to his writing, instead moving from book reading to book reading and checking on his online profiles via sites like StatCounter. He also uses social media to find out about the people he meets at parties, for example checking out a girl he meets by 'reading all four years of her Facebook wall' (Lin 2013: 109), while he and his friends engage in a 'grouplivetweet' (231) of a random movie while high on drugs, just to pass the time. The novel charts several of Paul's relationships, with the second half focusing on scenes involving Paul and Erin, who in one instance end up emailing each other even though they are actually in the same room. Elsewhere, Paul uses the phrase 'in-person conversation' (23) as though this is noteworthy, while the various parties result in an ongoing process of friending and defriending people with little sense of any real connection beyond the fleeting and the ephemeral.

Tao Lin's movement from social media and poetry to the novel may be yet another example of the ways in which writers still aspire to print publishing as the true mark of prestige and literary worth (discussed in Chapter 3). The problems besetting the Alt Lit movement might equally be seen as symptomatic of the toxicity that has ruined social media for so many, while the disappearance of several of its key figures could easily be seen as proof that perhaps there was really little of any lasting value here in the first place.

This chapter has provided a challenge to simplistic or utopian notions of community and suggested some of the ways in which abuses of power and influence can easily become amplified on social media. Nevertheless, the fact that so many influential literary networks depend for their very existence on social media is crucial in the context of the study as a whole in terms of trying to assess the significance of this particular cultural moment. Moreover, what is clear is that the idea of literature as something that can be generated collectively, shared, updated and customised readily across platforms and in ways beyond the control of its creators, is intrinsic, if not unique, to the specific cultures and subcultures of social media. The chapter has suggested some of the shared stylistic and structural features of work emerging from these collectivities, as well as pointing to the innovative ways in which they disseminate their work and engage with diverse audiences. The next chapter will go on to consider how more informal networks of writers, artists and readers rely for their existence on social media, as well as examining some of the new publishing platforms and shared activities that have emerged which blend the idea of the network with that of the market.

6   New literary cultures and markets

Previous chapters have outlined how social media facilitates the emergence of new kinds of writing, new kinds of authors, and new opportunities to participate in a wide range of activities contributing to the sense of some kind of shared literary culture. This chapter will explore in more depth how literary festivals, mass reading events and prizes engage with social media, and how social media has even generated its own literary events and award cultures. The chapter will also examine how the publishing and editing of literary works has become a social phenomenon with budding writers having ample opportunity to get feedback and advice on their work. In addition, the use of social media for marketing and promoting literary works and their authors will be examined. First, the chapter will focus on the role social media plays in connecting authors with their readers, and in making visible the various ways in which the authorial 'function' (Foucault 1991 [1969]) or brand is managed.

Authorship

As Myers (2016) has pointed out, taken in the context of celebrity culture on social media more generally, even the most high-profile authors such as J.K. Rowling rank pretty modestly. Nevertheless, for authors such as Joanne Harris who engage regularly with social media (Twitter, Tumblr, Facebook) there comes a time when the demands on authors and the expectations of readers need to be reassessed. So, in 2015 she published a 'Writer's Manifesto' setting out both what she pledged to do for her followers and what she will *not* do. Alongside this, followers of @Joannechocolat on Twitter are regularly reminded of where she draws the line in terms of her interactions with readers.

This kind of boundary drawing by authors can be risky. In the summer of 2019, Angie Thomas incurred a social media 'blowback' from the especially sensitive young adult book community when she appealed to readers *not* to tag authors when posting bad reviews of their work (Flood 2019). In another high profile case, Kathleen Hale went a stage further by tracking down and confronting an online reviewer who had adopted a fake persona to 'catfish' her (Hale 2014), resulting in accusations that she had overstepped the mark and become a 'crazy stalker' (Koul 2019) fundamentally threatening her whole writing career.

Of course book historians and fan scholars will rapidly remind us that authors have long engaged in book tours, performances of their work and correspondence with readers, but it is the 'unprecedented levels of abundance' that we now have for capturing and sharing 'authorial presence' (Kirschenbaum 2015) that is significant and new. As Kirschenbaum argues, this impacts not just on our perceptions of an author, but on our roles as literary critics, where a living author or his or her followers may easily push back against our interpretations and opinions and publicly challenge them. Moreover, it exacerbates the work that we as literary critics potentially have to do in tracking down authorial statements and in distinguishing them from their 'commingling' (Kirschenbaum 2015) with the views of fans and critics.

Maintaining a social media presence has become an expectation rather than an exception for contemporary authors, though many make a deliberate point of shunning social media, or express clear preferences in terms of particular platforms. Authors such as J.K. Rowling go further to use social media as a forum for social and political activism, as in her frequent dressings down for Donald Trump or her vocal support for the Remain campaign during the UK EU Referendum in 2016. Though she has been criticised for some of her comments she has defended her right to 'use my influence whatever way I want' (27 June 2016). Like Joanne Harris, Rowling does not shy away from responding to and confronting critical voices, and both use forthright language in defending their views even if that means losing followers or offending loyal readers.

How authors use social media has become a topic of interest and even debate. For example, in 2015 *The Guardian* published an article on '10 authors who excel on the internet' (Gwynne 2015) including those who primarily built their reputations via social media, such as Teju Cole (discussed in Chapter 3), as well as already established authors like Margaret Atwood and Salman Rushdie who have embraced social media for creative expression (Atwood) and to raise awareness of social and political issues (both Atwood and Rushdie). Equally, when an author shuts down his or her social media account, this can attract a lot of attention and debate. For example, Rushdie's dramatic 'abandonment' of his Twitter account in 2017 having lost patience with 'rude people' was widely reported (Shakespeare 2017).

Authors' use of social media can also be linked to a wider 'return to the social author' (Bold 2016) visible in the context of contemporary publishing infrastructures and practices, including the rise of authors whose very success depends on the work they put in building their unique brands, and developing their roles as social influencers. Bold argues that such opportunities appeal in particular to the 'long tail' of authors who may be neglected or even completely ignored by traditional publishers.

In her discussion of French digital authors' attitudes towards Facebook, Fülöp (2019) puts forward a typology based on authors who use, refuse and abuse the social network. Although her focus is on digital authors (i.e. those who write for digital platforms), she locates her discussion in the wider context of French ideas of the role of the 'auteur' and the conditions they face with regards to diminishing funds and the rigidity of the French publishing industry. In the case of digital authors, Fülöp argues that they nevertheless have to engage in forms of self-mediation and self-curation because this is bound up with the activity of producing literature in the digital space. She also considers how Facebook's terms and conditions impact on authors, restricting the extent to which they can use personal profiles for business, and the ways in which some of the digital authors try to circumvent this.

Murray's (2018) analysis of how authors use Twitter and other social media reveals how readers may develop a **parasocial** relationship with 'celebrity' authors who have taken over the cultivation of their public persona that would previously have been left to marketers and PR representatives. Even where an author appears to respond frequently to posts by followers, a glance at their profiles shows a huge disparity between the number of people following them and the number of people they (publicly) follow, highlighting the extent to which the perception that some kind of relationship exists is in the vast majority of cases illusory. The practice of 'doxxing' (revealing private or confidential information about someone online) represents the more malicious end of the spectrum, and sometimes is a direct response to the fact that certain individuals in the public eye refuse to engage and play the disclosure game. One of the most high profile cases involved the unmasking of the identity of the pseudonymous author Elena Ferrante in 2016, leading to a debate about the rights to privacy of authors but also revealing that readers may not always wish to know about the private lives of those who produce the works that move, affect and provoke them.

However, social media also provides an important network for authors, particularly up-and-coming authors keen to develop their reader base, celebrate landmarks such as publication day (#pubday) or share common writerly experiences such as seeing someone reading your book for the first time. Interaction between authors can provide illuminating insights into their reading and viewing habits and preferences, for example Stephen King's passion for the HBO show *Homeland*, or Margaret Atwood's support for various wildlife projects and environmental issues.

Clearly, therefore, authors' use of social media cannot be dismissed purely as publicity-seeking. Indeed, many authors give back just as much as they get out of exchanges with followers. In addition to her ad hoc comments on her art and career, Joanne Harris provides her followers with daily scheduled activities. In the morning, followers get an update on The Shed, her 'place of work; refuge and testing ground for dream machines' which 'changes shape and location daily', and which is only accessible to 'those bearing cake, or who already know where it is'. Other regular activities include #TenTweets, where Harris responds to suggestions from followers for example providing advice on responding to reviews or writing bestsellers. Meanwhile, the hashtag #Storytime alerts followers to a storytelling session about to unfold over successive tweets, while #CelebratingWomen provides snippets of information on lesser known women from history and the arts.

Ian McMillan's (@IMcmillan) UK-based followers share a special connection with the poet if they are also early risers who are active on Twitter. As one user puts it, they 'enjoy having a virtual twitter tea with you each morning' (11 October 2018). McMillan shares regular updates on visits by his grandchildren, the fortunes of Barnsley F.C., his mother-in-law's meat and tattie pies and his Sunday ritual of preparing the Yorkshire Pudding. His son, the poet Andrew McMillan (@AndrewPoetry) is also active on Twitter, and occasionally father and son exchange messages. McMillan senior regularly interacts with poets including Michael Rosen and Lemn Sissay and shares in activities with his followers. For example, on the first of September in 2018 he and his followers exchanged short poems incorporating his name in various Beatle songs. McMillan has long been a familiar figure to television and radio audiences in the UK, and as a performer of his poetry. Quotations on his website (3 September 2018) describe him as 'jovial', 'democratic' and 'inspiring', helping to explain his popularity and the clear feeling amongst his followers that he is someone who is likely to be approachable. In 2018, McMillan published a book based on his collected #WitandWisdom from Twitter. However, unlike some of the authors discussed in Chapter 3, this is not so much a graduation from social media to print for McMillan as he is already established as a print poet, and the book is very much marketed as a novelty item rather than a contribution to his oeuvre.

The setting of tasks or challenges for followers is another authorial device which can create a sense of interaction without their having to engage directly with each and every user. In Februrary 2018 Claire Fuller (@ClaireFuller2) collaborated with The Reading Agency, a charity devoted to promoting reading in the UK, and the publisher Penguin Books, to invite people to share stories about the strangest things they had found in books. The prize was a copy of *Swimming Lessons* by Fuller, in which one of the main characters collects books for the things readers have left and written in them. Fuller helped to publicise the competition via her Twitter account and retweeted several of the entries. In this case, the activity not only drew on but even appeared to provide an extension of the fictional world created by Fuller, allowing followers to connect their own experiences to those featured in the novel.

Such activities demonstrate how on social media the lines between marketing and mutually enriching social interaction can be hard to define. Nothing is more exciting and empowering for a reader than to feel they are being personally addressed by an author whose work they admire, but often on social media this can seem like little more than a ruse to open up the lines of communication only to bombard them with promotional material. Alert to this, for the publication of her follow up book to *Swimming Lessons, Bitter Orange*, Fuller tweeted photographs of herself at various book signings, but was careful to apologise to followers for the seeming self-promotion on the basis that 'You can just count to ten and they will have come and gone. That is the nature of Twitter' (3 August, 2018).

In addition to maintaining a regular presence on Twitter, as 'writer-clairefuller', Fuller posts photographs and bookstagrams featuring her own works and those of others on Instagram. Mark Haddon (mjphaddon) posts photographs and artwork on Instagram, while Joanne Harris maintains an account on Tumblr and also uses crowdfunding sites such as Ko-fi. This demonstrates how many authors are keen to seek out readers but also to actively generate communities across platforms. Moreover, it reinforces the idea of authors as avid readers and bookish people themselves, passionate about the act of reading but equally interested in books as objects and commodities that can be worked into various kinds of visual or multimodal displays.

I have written previously about the phenomenon of the 'trickster author' (Thomas 2011c) who haunts the online forums where readers come together to discuss his or her work. On social media we can see at a glance who authors are following or who they retweet, but this does not account for the phenomenon of 'lurking' where they may be observing or listening in on others' discussions covertly. It is perhaps not surprising that writers, who typically work in isolation, should seek out social contact. One of the seeming benefits of social media is that they can choose when to take a break, and how long to engage with other users for, though clearly there are instances when seemingly banal exchanges escalate into heated discussions or generate threads made up of multiple variations on a theme. For writers like Joanne Harris, who campaigns on behalf of authors and against commercial piracy and casual exploitation, social media can be used to issue rallying calls to other authors to join in the fight. In the UK in Spring 2018, several authors including Harris came out in support of The Reading Agency's Quick Reads campaign which had been halted due to lack of funding. Similarly, the hashtag #AuthorsAssemble was used in March 2018 to help publicise the work of the Society of Authors in the face of low incomes and decreasing royalties for authors, with many authors posting selfies or shelfies in support.

As well as assembling to counteract injustice, authors use hashtags to share the experience of writing and being a writer. Perhaps the most well-known is #amwriting which is used widely by authors, academics and others not just to record activity but as a motivational aid. A common activity is to recount the number of words written in a day, or to share the various stumbling blocks and distractions that get in the way of writing. In some instances, authors are candid about their need to start generating income, and the personal or professional difficulties they face. In the Spring of 2018, the topic of working-class representation in UK publishing sparked discussion of careers in the industry, as well as the barriers faced by writers who struggle to pay for promotional materials, agents and the like. One of the triggers for this discussion was the launch of a crowdfunding campaign on www.unbound.com for Kit de Waal's *Common People*, and the establishment of a working-class writers' collective inspired by the project.

The insights provided by social media into the daily routines and writing practices of authors provides a potentially rich resource which is publicly available to researchers and, as discussed in Chapter 4, relatively easy to capture and quantify with the kinds of tools for scraping social media data. From poet Ian McMillan's daily reflections on his 'early strolls' to Stephen King's whimsical updates on 'Molly aka Thing of Evil' (who has her own Facebook profile), it could perhaps be argued that this kind of information panders to the celebrification of the author and the voyeuristic impulses of followers. However, it could equally be said to demystify the figure of the author by showing how their lives 'jostle' with their works (Braun and Spiers 2016), and can be a means for authors to manage and control their relations with their readers.

Providing readers with constant updates on progress and updates to works in progress is a feature I have previously identified and analysed in relation to fanfiction (Thomas 2011a). The implications of this extend not just to the concept of authorship as something much more collaborative and dependent on interaction but also to the idea of the 'work' itself as something which is subject to revision, detours and sidetracks, rather than as something which comes forth fully formed from the mind of the creative genius whose name it carries.

The experience of following an author over months and years on social media can lead to the kinds of parasocial relationships discussed by Murray (2018). However, it may equally provide readers with valuable insights into the everyday lives of authors and how authorial careers evolve, stutter or change track over time. As Dix (2017) contends, literary criticism tends to focus on individual works or periods rather than on the concept of the career and the pressures that authors may face producing the second or third work in a series, or replicating the success they may have had earlier in their careers. Following the social media accounts of established authors can reveal how they view their public personae, how they deal with celebrity, and how they perceive their own status in relation to their contemporaries. Employing tools such as social network analysis (discussed in Chapter 4) may further offer interesting insights into which authors follow each other or comment on or retweet each other's posts. Interaction *between* authors may also become visible as they share knowing remarks about the demands placed upon them, or demonstrate their solidarity with one another in the face of lack of understanding, misconceptions and myths from those outside their circle, for example by joining in with popular hashtags like #amwriting.

Of course, in addition to spoof accounts for both dead and living authors, many author accounts are patently there for promotion rather than interaction. News of latest releases and links to product pages are common. American author Mark Danielewski regularly features merchandise such as hoodies or t-shirts featuring quotations from his novels, as well as involving followers in competitions and games where they can contribute content for existing or future works. In January 2016, Laura McVeigh (@lcmcveigh) even successfully pitched a book idea via Twitter, securing a contract for *Under The Almond Tree* after being taken on by Jonny Geller from the Curtis Brown agency.

As well as these overt activities, authors may operate more covertly, for example using algorithms or hashtags to track down potential readers or following multiple random accounts as a means of promoting their own work. As @onlinereaders1 I have had many experiences of being followed on Twitter by authors who presumably pick out my account based on mentions of readers or reading. The profiles of these authors often link directly to purchase options for their most recent books, thus providing something akin to a direct selling experience where it is the person responsible for producing that work who corresponds and communicates with the potential consumer.

In other instances, however, authorship may be less easily attributable, and the question of exactly who is responsible for the creation and dissemination of material may be much more complex. For example, in the case of @Hooklandguide, (discussed earlier in Chapter 2), the account profile takes us to @cultauthor 'David Southwell', whose Wikipedia entry describes him as an author of bestselling books on conspiracy theories and organised crime. However, the world of Hookland also alludes frequently to the writings of 'CL Nolan' described as a 'folklorist, broadcaster, strange story writer, former fighter against pirates in the Strait of Malacca'. Moreover, as an alternative folk history and collective hallucination Hookland relies on followers to expand its traditions, rituals and customs. Followers' contributions to the 'guide' keep close to the house style and respond to new avenues for 'studies' and research suggested by others. In May 2018 the hashtag #VOH (Voice of Hookland) was used for a series of quotations from various Hooklanders including the evocatively named John Gaunt and Mal Parkin.

The concept of authorship in this regard takes us down the kind of rabbit hole (Thomas 2014b) we frequently encounter in web-based storytelling, where the boundaries between real-life and fictional authors or creators is often blurred. It also contributes to a return to the idea of authorship as a collaborative activity discussed in Chapter 5, though not necessarily at the expense of the notion of the 'private voice' as Myers (2016) has claimed. However, the concept of intellectual property and ownership of creative content (discussed briefly in Chapter 1) becomes especially problematic where that content is spread across different media or accessed via different platforms, and where content can be modified, added to or removed by others. This helps explain why authors such as Joanne Harris speak out about the need to recognise writing as a profession, and writers as people who need to get paid for their labour. Moreover, it ties in with debates about the exploitation of labour in online spaces outlined in the Introduction.

As well as interacting with living authors, social media provides a space for readers to commemorate the births and deaths of authors, or other notable dates from their timelines. This can manifest itself in reproducing quotations accompanied by photographs or other contextual detail, as in the following tweet from writer and poet @SorayaBhakhbakhi commemorating Sylvia Plath's birthday (27 October):

Sylvia Plath, one of my most beloved poets and writers, was born on this day in 1932:
"The blood jet is poetry,
There is no stopping it."

#OnThisDay #Poet #Poetry #Quote #Poem #Birthday #Sylvia Plath #Books #Literature

The original tweet also featured three photographs of Plath, arranged as a kind of triptych, while the tags increase the tweet's discoverability for other users. In particular, the hashtag #OnThisDay (often abbreviated as OTD) is widely used to link content to key historical or cultural events. In many instances, these commemorative acts are reminiscent of the phenomenon of fan pilgrimages (Zubernis and Larsen 2018) as they often carry with them a sense of devotion and remembrance of a quasi-religious kind.

However, the activity may prompt more complex responses, particularly where the legacy of the author in question may be the subject of controversy, for example @chaletfan's double-edged tribute to Enid Blyton on the anniversary of her birth (11 August 2019): 'Happy Birthday Enid Blyton, you crazy sausage of contradiction, everything isms, and rampant brutality, you. (I do love her but man, she's a strange old bean.)'

Fans, amateurs and reader–writers

In her 'Manifesto', Harris (2015) is critical of the ways in which the idea that 'we're all authors now' threatens to obscure the extent to which so many professional authors work hard for little material reward. However, at the same time she frequently displays her knowledge and interest in fan cultures and fanfiction as providing a space for experimentation and play. For some, including Harris, perhaps an important distinction remains between writers and authors, whether that distinction is simply drawn in terms of the extent to which an individual is able to base a career on his or her writing, or in terms of the extent to which what they produce is seen as of lasting value, or is original or groundbreaking in some way.

Other terms have also emerged that attempt to redefine authorship for the social media age. The term 'demotic author' is used by Skains (2019) to refer to a kind of writing which emerges from the everyday and which engages with the popular rather than positioning itself in opposition to it. In fan studies, Scott (2013) has coined the term 'fanboy auteur' to refer to creative artists who align themselves with specific fandoms or engage more broadly with fan cultures. In the context of transmedia storytelling, the terms czar, curator and steward (Dena 2009) have all been employed to manoeuvre around the complex ways in which the creators of these worlds work not just across texts and platforms, but often with multiple collaborators, making any discussion around the ownership, origin or hierarchy of individual elements highly problematic.

In her discussion of contemporary literature and digital publishing, Vadde (2017) focuses more broadly on the various kinds of 'amateur creativity' found across the internet and social media, and the ways in which digital publishing has led to 'mass amateurization of the critical, creative and communicative arts' (27). Vadde, like Skains, draws extensively on Lessig's (2008: 28) concept of the '**Read-Write**' culture in which amateurs can contribute to an increasingly 'free culture' (144) in contemporary writing, though Vadde is critical of the fact that the potential for exploitation is absent from Lessig's analysis. Taking a sociological approach, Vadde, like Skains, sees fan cultures and web platforms devoted to fandoms as inspiring professional writers to 'break with the "literary" mold' (30). In particular, Vadde associates this with a rejection of 'individualist conceptions of authorship, the excesses of celebrity culture, the economy of prestige, and market-circumscribed attempts to monetize cultural wealth' (30). While debates about the quality or lasting value of amateur creative activities such as fanfiction continue, for many critics such as Vadde and Skains, they offer a useful corrective to mainstream publishing in terms of the diversity of participants, and the ways in which identity, hierarchy and status are fluid rather than givens.

Literary advice

Harris's (2015) 'Manifesto' also recognises how self-publishing, ebooks and fanfiction have made it possible for more and more people to share but also get feedback and advice on their writing. Fanfiction sites in particular have provided a supportive environment for writers where sharing updates and work in progress may be more highly valued than offering polished end products (Thomas 2011a). Fanfiction communities have often been perceived positively in this regard as spaces where diverse tastes and practices can be accommodated, and where more experienced writers freely give of their time and expertise as **beta readers**.

In addition to this kind of peer-to-peer advice, numerous social media accounts exist (e.g. @AdvicetoWriters on Twitter) dedicated to sharing motivational quotations from established authors, providing insights into their creative practices or reflecting on what it means to be an author. Online spaces and social media therefore together offer the kind of support that writers might previously have expected from writing workshops, editors or literary agents, often with no upfront cost, no contract or long-term commitment, and with unlimited access to resources.

Of course, it would once again be dangerous to overstate how new this all is. To some extent, aspiring writers have always been able to find outlets for their creativity, as well as plenty of advice as to how to improve and hone their writing skills. Hilliard (2006) has charted the various manifestations of the 'literary advice industry' since the 1880s, and specific historical, social and cultural turning points or events that have helped give impetus to new writing, for example the increased emphasis on creative writing in the school curriculum in the post-war years. Hilliard's study shows how the emergence of literary magazines allowed writers to not only publish their work, but to derive an income from their writing. In addition, he demonstrated how writers' circles, far from being confined to Bloomsbury or the affluent suburbs, catered to the thirst and desire to write and share one's writing from individuals from across the social spectrum and from a variety of educational backgrounds.

Then, as now, the dream of becoming a writer can easily be exploited. Yet in the vast majority of instances online and on social media, resources are offered freely, most often than not on a peer-to-peer basis, rather than as top-down advice from an expert. Much like the gift economy of fan communities, advice is offered in good faith, interspersed among the user's other daily contributions, in a spirit of reciprocity. However, debates continue as to whether or not this kind of 'affective labor' (Martens 2016) is little more than a system set up to exploit willing 'Net Slaves' (Terranova 2000: 33). In her study of the 'Random Buzzers' website set up for teen readers by the publisher Random House, Martens observes how participants do not just post messages or complete games and quizzes but engage in social networking. This book-related labour that the teens engage in offers a rich source of data which can be exploited by publishers and others. Nevertheless, Martens argues that the young readers and reviewers can gain cultural capital by developing and displaying their expertise, as well as providing them with access to a vast repertoire of information, knowledge and advice on their favourite authors.

Wattpad, 'the world's largest community for readers and writers' replicates much of the reciprocal ethos of fanfiction sites, with constant invites to the browser to 'try your hand at writing', and 'be part of the experience' (www.wattpad.com May 2018), and through its constant address to the user as both reader *and* writer. As with Martens' study, the Wattpad community is also predominantly made up of teens and young adults. Wattpad brands itself as a space for writing that provides a 'social, on-the-go experience', its design and visual imagery aimed at a young audience interested in accessing but also creating stories on their smartphones. In her study of Wattpad, Davies (2017) maintains that

80% of the user base is thirty or under and that 90% of interactions take place through mobile devices. One of the biggest success stories of Wattpad is Anna Todd's 300-chapter story based on the boy band One Direction, feeding into the fantasy that writers and writing talent can be discovered in the most unlikely of places (Todd's day jobs included working in a waffle house). As Laquintano (2016) and Davies (2017) have both pointed out, an important part of this fantasy is that the writer should ultimately progress to print, with Wattpad being seen very much as a stepping stone on the road to success. In early 2019, Wattpad announced that it was setting up its own publishing division, using the 'data-driven' opinions of readers and users as its starting point, but combining this with the expertise of human editors (de León 2019), consolidating the notion of heightened prestige and status for print, and providing further evidence of the extent to which writers on social media may have to look to more traditional outlets to consolidate and develop their careers, as discussed previously in Chapter 3.

Alongside the fannish sensibility, and sometimes in contradiction with it, advice on Wattpad is directed towards writing as a business, with tips about how to make your stories stand out or how to use social media to network with other writers and readers. This advice can be sourced on the site from blogs and forums, and Wattpad encourages engagement with a wider community via links to social media, including Twitter, Facebook, Instagram and YouTube. Moreover, a whole new market has grown to cater for 'wattpadders' keen to further develop their skills, for example *The Writer's Guide to Wattpad* (Sobieck 2018), an ebook promising 'behind the scenes' insights, as well as countless interviews and features with Wattpad success stories. With its culture of Wattpad 'Stars' and competitions, much of the advice and guidance is directed towards success measured in terms of popularity and commercial appeal. But this is complemented by a focus on audience building and retention, for example advice to 'post one chapter at a time', 'post regularly' and to maintain regular interaction with readers. The site design and focus on sociality replicates the browsing experience described by Weedon (2007) in her study of internet book spaces, where users help each other to discover content and shared pleasures, but where the design is equally about keeping browsers on the site to ensure advertising revenue, much as physical bookstores may provide sofas, coffee or events to attract consumers.

Both Vadde (2017) and Skains (2019) have explored how Wattpad acts as a kind of training ground for aspiring writers, drawing links with the cultures of sharing and mutual support from fan sites. Furthermore, Vadde considers how professional writers such as Margaret Atwood have used the platform for new ventures (Atwood's collaboration with

Naomi Alderman on *The Happy Zombie Sunrise Home*) and connects this to wider trends in terms of cultural practices, notably the popularity of serialised content. Vadde goes on to question the notion that Wattpad might represent the kind of 'transnationally networked free culture' (2017: 40) advocates such as Atwood might claim for it, arguing instead for a more modest facility to provide opportunities for 'tryout' and 'recoding'.

Regardless of whether we see these spaces as exploitative or supportive, what they undoubtedly offer is unprecedented access to the creative process and its reception. Thus, on fanfiction sites and on Wattpad, we can follow a piece of writing through from inception to publication and revision, and learn about the strategies writers use to publicise and market their work and to build dedicated readerships. Online and social media writing communities also potentially challenge the dominance and restrictive practices of publishers and the literary industry, leading not only to greater opportunities for producing, discovering and circulating literary works, but also for greater numbers of people to become involved in those processes, whether as editors, writers, or patrons of new writing.

New publishing models

The rise of self-publishing and the vast opportunities seemingly available to writers in the digital era have led to renewed debates about the commercialisation of literature and the need for traditional gatekeepers tasked with maintaining standards. As discussed previously, they have also helped to both perpetuate myths of authorship, particularly that of the undiscovered genius, and to demystify the writing process, where writers may engage with their readers and share their creative journeys, even responding to feedback and suggestions for content. While self-publishing has historically been perceived negatively at least in relation to literary writing, according to Levey (2016), in the digital age self-publishing may give authors more freedoms and control over their work, particularly those aspects such as marketing and distribution that would previously have been costed in to their contracts with their publishers.

Social media facilitates a kind of self-publishing in the sense that users can post content which will be immediately accessible to a potentially vast audience. We saw in Chapter 3 how this works specifically with regards to literary content posted on Twitter. To amplify the reach of posts, users may also choose to tag content through the use of hashtags (as in the case of #LossLit), or by means of a collective account (@terriblytiny). In many cases too, content produced for websites, blogs etc. may be linked to and publicised via social media. Thus even where social media is not the primary or sole source or container for published content, it plays an important role, not least as the language of sharing, following and liking shapes and defines how users access, distribute and evaluate that content.

Numerous apps and websites now provide aspiring writers with the opportunity to not only publish their work, but to build their networks and connect with readers. For example, Czech based app Poetizer claims to make it easy for users 'to discover, celebrate, and share poems with the world'. The app is free and users can sign up via Facebook, Twitter, Google or email. Curation and hierarchisation appear minimal: users choose either to access poems in terms of recency or via a 'Newsfeed'. Yet the reality is that any presentation and framing of content in this way inevitably introduces forms of intermediation and hierarchisation, for example the fact that Poetizer's 'Top Poems' are selected based on the number of views or likes. In addition, almost invariably, platforms and communities such as Poetizer will have stringent terms and conditions, as well as administrators and moderators who will not only decide what content is posted, but how and where (Thomas and Round 2016).

In some cases, this intermediation may not appear that different from traditional forms of literary publishing. As discussed in Chapter 1, in the 1980s, Eastgate systems emerged as an online publisher for hypertext fiction, acting as an intermediary between writers and readers, and providing the latter with access to hypertext fiction in the form of floppy disks and CDs. Somewhat incongruously in the context of the euphoria about the emergence of new media writing in this period and the embrace of the world wide web as a libertarian space, Eastgate charged for content, and in some cases restricted that content in terms of the formats available. Eastgate was, and still is, both publisher and retailer, but it presented itself very much as a purveyor of 'serious' fiction.

Likewise, online literary magazines often look back to a long tradition aimed at a highbrow readership. McSweeney's Internet Tendency is a non-profit venture drawing on the success and notoriety of the publishing company of the same name set up by Dave Eggers in 1998. It 'exists to champion ambitious and inspired new writing and to challenge conventional expectations about where it's found, how it looks, and who participates' (www.mcsweeneys.net) and as well as an online book store, the website has links to the *Timothy McSweeney's Quarterly Concern* literary journal. With its close association with Eggers, this publishing model can be located in a long tradition of the publishing house associate with, or in some cases run by, successful literary authors. Meanwhile, online magazine *Pendora* (which folded in 2019) set out its preference for writing with a 'strong sense of aesthetic, innovative fiction, non-fiction focus on the Self: literature concerned with memory and personal experiences, which strip away elements of conventional fiction in order to reveal a genuine truth within the author's Self'. Alongside original writing, the website featured reviews, essays and artwork.

In contrast, the vast majority of today's writing spaces and publishing models appear more concerned with popularity and monetising content than innovation and the avant garde. Much like Wattpad, Terribly Tiny Tales (@terriblytiny) provides ways for aspiring writers to post content, get feedback and build followers via its app, website and social media. However, it also encourages writers to apply for 'Select' status by taking a copy test, allows users to commission 'Tailored Tales', and has a YouTube channel featuring short films made by its 'terribly tiny talkies' collective (which users can apply to join).

While Wattpad and Terribly Tiny Tales define themselves as a community that supports new writing, other ventures, like Eastgate, seem to base their models much more around familiar structures from traditional publishing, but combining these with models and practices emerging from the attention and gig economies. For example, online publishers such as Unbound and Wet Zebra have developed a crowdfunding model to provide authors with many of the services associated with traditional publishing (for example book launches), but leaving the decision about which projects get published to readers who get to vote on extracts or samples of the work in progress. Wet Zebra distinguishes between writers (who are 'wet') and authors (whose works are available to buy). Describing themselves as 'democratic' publishers, they nevertheless include several well-known authors and public figures on their lists. In addition, some of the 'team' double as authors, strongly suggesting that recognisability is an important factor in raising one's profile and attracting votes on the site.

The dominant narratives perpetuated by these publishers is that of bypassing the elitist and corporate-driven mainstream, offering a more democratic model based on the choices and preferences of real readers. So instead of employing a literary agent to negotiate a contract, writers pitch their ideas direct to their potential readers to invite pledges from supporters until they hopefully reach their target and get their work published. In their preface to the 'Poet Laureate of Twitter' Brian Bilston's *You Took the Last Bus Home* (discussed in Chapter 3), which was published by Unbound in 2016, 'Dan, Justin and John', the founders of the company, claim that their model is based on 'a very old idea', referring back to Samuel Johnson's publication of his dictionary. They further claim that their model frees authors 'to write the books they really want', while at the same time liberating readers who are no longer to be seen as 'passive consumers' (Bilston 2016).

In 2017 I interviewed Tim Wright, an interactive media producer and digital writer who, along with his collaborator Lloyd Shepherd, had pitched on Unbound but just fell short of the target (Wright 2017). Despite the fact that the project did not get funded, Tim was very complimentary about the support offered by Unbound. He acknowledged that the project in question, which involved some complicated transmedia elements, may have suffered from the fact that it lacked an immediate 'recognition factor' which he felt would be particularly helpful in a situation where quick judgements are being made. He noted, however, that the process was still ultimately reliant on the judgement of the publisher (who has to be persuaded by the project before it can go onto the site), and that the makeup of the community is largely 'booky people'. He also reflected that despite the fact that Unbound had provided excellent services, the overheads they imposed (compared to independent digital production) made the target difficult to reach. This was from someone very experienced at obtaining project funding, demonstrating that the notion that such platforms make it possible for anyone to pursue their dream of becoming a writer can sometimes be at odds with the reality.

While some of these crowdfunding ventures and online writing communities are very much based on finding and promoting individual writing talent, similar models exist which focus more broadly on 'stories', thus allowing creative teams to form, bringing varied talents and skillsets to work collaboratively on multimedia or transmedia creations. In 2018 a former student of mine from Bournemouth University was part of a campaign on Seed&Spark to fund a web series called Rational Creatures which reimagines Jane Austen's *Persuasion* through a series of vlogs based around the goal of boosting inclusivity particularly with regards to gender, ethnicity and sexuality. In keeping with other crowdfunding sites, the model allows funders to get involved in a variety of ways and to feel that they are sharing in the development of the project rather than merely bankrolling it into existence.

In many instances, therefore, new publication models do not so much break new ground as return us to older practices and models, particularly that of private literary patronage. For example, McSweeney's Internet Tendency invites readers to continue to 'support writers and keep our site ad-free' through donating via Patreon, an online crowdfunding membership platform. Nevertheless, Feng's (2012) study of the vast market for online literature in China showed that the relationship between patrons and creators in the digital era can be more complex. She demonstrates how some key features of the Chinese market distinguish it from online Western communities, particularly the levying of a fee for entering certain parts of the website. But she also argues that the communities that formed around these spaces are able to 'foster emotional nurturance, explore gender identities and test their creative voices' (49). The erection of paywalls in the Chinese context may need to be contextualised specifically with regard to offering protection to users from state censorship. In addition, while it may be hard to ignore the commercial realities of targeting readers 'as a profit-generating consumer base' (50), on Chinese fan sites upgrading in fact buys readers certain privileges, allowing them to negotiate content with authors tailored to their own preferences.

In April 2019, Wattpad introduced a 'Paid Stories' option for users, offering exclusivity and 'seamless reading' for purchasers. Paid Stories (developed in beta as 'Wattpad Next') thus provides another iteration of literary patronage where the transaction between reader and writer appears direct and unmediated, and where the emphasis is on mutual benefit. Alongside Wattpad's introduction of a publishing imprint, Wattpad Books, and Wattpad Studios which 'works with media executives to single out stories that have a great chance of commercial success', this marks a decisive shift away from the gift economy of fanfiction.

As discussed in the Introduction, many social media platforms (YouTube, Tumblr) have developed models whereby users now routinely expect pay for additional, enhanced or personalised content in various ways. Easily dismissed as examples of commercialisation and exploitation, nevertheless they raise important questions about the extent to which patronage and support for the arts can be rewarding and mutually enriching, and in some instances can offer opportunities for participation for users that might not otherwise arise.

Festivals and prizes

Festivals and prizes represent another aspect of the literary industry that brings to the foreground, uncomfortably for some, questions around patronage, hierarchies and commerciality. They feature prominently in the literary calendar and publishers' schedules as opportunities to raise the profile of authors and/or their works and also as opportunities to connect with readers. However, the extent to which lesser known writers and smaller publishers may be priced out of participation has become part of a wider debate to do with lack of diversity in the industry, at least in the UK. Festivals and prizes may also be said to contribute to the celebrification of literature, both in the sense of giving pride of place to established celebrities from the world of entertainment who dominate book sales, and in the sense of pressure on writers to become more 'mediagenic' (Todd 1996: 60). At the same time, festivals and prizes contribute to the idea that notions of taste and quality are becoming democratised to include readers and audiences, particularly with the popularity of 'meet the author' sessions and people's votes. In his study of the impact of the Booker Prize in the UK, English (2005) on the one hand links the 'prize frenzy' of the 1980s to the entrepreneurial ideology of the Thatcher period, but on the other sees the potential dissolution of the opposition between cultural and economic capital as set out by Bourdieu and others in much more positive terms.

High profile literary festivals and prizes now routinely make use of social media to promote events and to invite participation through competitions, voting and so on. Moreover, they rely on online spaces for archiving materials, generating new content, and as a means to include book bloggers and ebook authors on panels or video link-ups (Weber 2018). Online spaces can also benefit established festivals by allowing them the flexibility to respond to emerging book cultures and new audiences (Driscoll 2015; Weber 2018).

For smaller festivals, social media can be invaluable for reaching out to audiences beyond the immediate geographical area, and for managing some of the day to day business including programming and ticketing. For example, the Llandeilo Lit Fest in South Wales uses Facebook and Twitter (@LlandeiloLitFst) to publicise events, share news and images and videos with followers. In cases such as these, the digital and live experiences complement each other because literary audiences are so used to forming communities across diverse platforms (Weber 2018).

Festivals have emerged that directly respond to the kinds of literary activity generated by and existing in online spaces and social media, for example the Twitterfiction festival discussed in Chapter 3. Similarly, in Australia, the Digital Writers' Festival has become a standalone event having previously been a strand of the long-established Melbourne Emerging Writers' Festival (Weber 2018). Meanwhile, for researchers of festivals, digital tools such as sentiment analysis (discussed in Chapter 4) allow for greater recognition of the role of emotional engagement for audiences (Driscoll 2015).

Literary prizes likewise rely on social media for generating anticipation, while authors and their publishers in contention for prizes turn to social media to press their case and elicit support. For example, Salman Rushdie abandoned his abandonment of Twitter to celebrate the shortlisting of his novel *Quichotte* for the 2019 Booker Prize. For the bigger prizes like the Booker, book bloggers may provide text and visual commentary on unfolding events, and of course social media provides a forum for readers to register their opinions and views on the judges' choices.

Prizes specific to social media also exist. The Blooker Prize, an award for books based on blogs (or 'blooks'), was set up by the online self-publishing company Lulu.com and ran in 2006 and 2007 with Cory Doctorow as one of the judges. Meanwhile, the 'Shorty Awards' which 'honor the best of social media' has a category specifically for the 'best in literature' (https://shortyawards.com/category/10th/literature) celebrating original outputs. A previous winner of this award, Arjun Basu was discussed in Chapter 3. In 2018 an award for self-published authors (The Selfie) was launched by Book Brunch, a daily online news service for the book industry in association with the London Book Fair (www. theselfies.co.uk). In addition to the demand for a 'fantastic story' the criteria for the £1,000 award included an 'effective and creative marketing and publication strategy'. The setting up of the award in part responds to criticism of other high-profile awards for lack of diversity and for excluding or sidelining self-published works. Moreover, it suggests that self-publishing is emerging more as a deliberate choice for some authors rather than a route forced on them by rejection from mainstream publishers.

The Goodreads Choice awards, 'the only major book awards decided by readers' according to their website, has numerous categories for members to vote on. Writing in *The Washington Post*, Charles (2018) acknowledges the controversies that the sheer number of categories and voting practices of fans has created, but asks whether 'the best measure of the legitimacy of a book prize is the vibrancy of the discussion it inspires'. Charles notes that women writers feature prominently in the list of recipients of the awards, and he suggests that these awards perhaps tell us more about the age we live in than about the books themselves. Certainly, the Goodreads awards do prompt discussion and debate not just about the winners and losers but also about the awards process and extent to which divisions between genre writing and literature can still be sustained or subscribed to in terms of assumptions about quality, aesthetic beauty or the like.

Nevertheless, while online awards are gaining attention, as discussed in earlier chapters, there is still a sense in which authors and critics ascribe greater credibility to more established awards deriving from older print or media cultures. Thus, in April 2019 it was still considered noteworthy that Lindsey Ellis, a creator of YouTube video essays, was nominated for the Hugo Award (Vorel 2019). Recognising the best science fiction and fantasy writing since the 1950s, the Hugo Awards are themselves testament to changing taste cultures with regards to genre fiction. Although Ellis was not the first YouTuber to be nominated, her series of essays on the 'Hobbit Duology' examining the background to the Peter Jackson adaptations of Tolkein's novel appears to have been widely perceived as an incremental advance over the achievements of Rachel Bloom for her nomination for the music video 'Fuck Me, Ray Bradbury' in 2010.

Mass reading events

Alongside literary festivals, mass reading events have become another regular feature of the literary calendar allowing readers to connect with authors and each other. Fuller and Rehberg Sedo (2013) have written about the influence of mass reading events on contemporary reading cultures, particularly 'One Book, One Chicago' and 'Canada Reads'. This focus on book reading as a social experience rooted in specific communities has been very influential on studies of social reading in the digital age. The idea of participating in a shared reading 'event' crosses over into the digital through activities such as online 'group reads' (Thomas and Round 2016) and social media 'readalongs' (discussed in Chapter 2). Rather like the phenomenon of 'event television', clearly an important part of the experience provided by such activities is that of being in the moment with other readers, whether that experience is of encountering a new text, or revisiting an old favourite. Much has been written about the phenomenon of 'second screening' with regards to watching television in this way, but far less attention has been paid to the various means by which readers turn to social media to connect with others, share and reflect on their reading, *while* they are engaged in reading.

Reader power

In the preceding sections we have seen how, thanks to social media, readers are moving very much into the foreground of the contemporary literary scene, interacting with authors, voting online for crowdfunded publishing ventures and diverse prizes, and engaging in festivals and mass reading events. No longer taken for granted or relegated to the shadows, readers are constantly being addressed, invited to participate and held up as figures whose opinions really do seem to matter.

In her manifesto response to what she perceived as a 'false sense of entitlement' from some of her readers, Joanne Harris (2015) may appear to be espousing the rebuilding of the barricades between writers and readers that the internet and social media appeared to have overthrown. However, designed as a 'provocation', underlying Harris's manifesto is a frustration with the lack of respect (and rewards) afforded to writers in an age when it appears 'anyone' can publish. In addition, if there is disdain, it is disdain for simplistic tools purporting to give readers more choice rather than disdain for those readers themselves.

As discussed in Chapter 1, the rise of electronic literature and interactive narratives led to an often celebratory rhetoric around the concept of a hybrid figure of a 'wreader', while in fan cultures reading or viewing has become closely associated with a kind of activism extending far beyond the fictional world, to impact on real life issues such as sexuality or bullying. Thus, we have groups such as The Harry Potter Alliance (www.thehpalliance.org) emerging to 'make activism accessible through the power of story', enlisting fans to help campaign and 'join the cause' and set up their own local chapters.

Social media further facilitates access to other readers and makes visible the interactions that take place between them, whether that is discussions on online book recommendation sites such as Goodreads, or activities taking place in online forums and book groups. Across social media, individuals self-identify as readers and follow hashtags that serve to assemble groups or subgroups for readers to join. One of the most popular bookish tags on Twitter and Instagram is #amreading, allowing users to record their reading activities and to reach out to others currently reading the same book or who have previously read it, facilitating discussion and a sense of incorporating the private act of reading into an activity that is more social. As discussed in Chapter 2, hashtags can also be used more playfully, to prompt game-like collaborative activities or set challenges for followers. Hashtags can also be used to raise the profile of reading by organisations and charities promoting literacy: in 2016 The Reading Agency encouraged readers to record the books that got them into reading by using the hashtag #childofbooks.

As well as performing the function of tagging talk and making it easier for users to find content related to a particular subject, hashtags perform an interpersonal role and help users to enact certain identities (Zappavigna 2014) providing a sense of an 'ambient audience' who are always there, always listening. In the case of readers, this could arguably be said to have gained new impetus in an age when reading is perceived to be under threat. In his discussion of 'Book Twitter', Matt Coleman (2018) describes social media spaces as 'the high school lunchroom we book loners have coveted all our lives', his language suggesting that 'book loners', rather like fans, may perceive themselves as marginalised, misunderstood but nevertheless resilient.

The hashtag #wethereaders which appeared around 2015 seemed to give voice to a reading formation (Bennett and Woollacott 1987) bordering on a social movement, echoed by other rallying calls (#beareader) and expressions of defiance or militancy (#ireadeverywhere). However, #wethereaders was in fact part of a promotional campaign for Kindle India, and is symptomatic of another tendency observable across social media, which speaks to the reader as consumer, offering us the opportunity to express and pronounce our readerliness to others by buying t-shirts, tote bags or other merchandise with references to reading or readers emblazoned across them.

In her discussion of 'citizen critics', Eberly (2000) recounts how ordinary readers have for decades influenced the public sphere and offered an alternative to the promotional cultures including reviews managed by publishing companies. However, not everyone is enthused by the ways in which this activity has accelerated in the digital age. In 2006, the subject of book bloggers provoked a furious exchange between critic John Sutherland and novelist Susan Hill (Lea 2006). Sutherland's complaint was that web reviewers 'enjoy shooting off their mouths' leading Hill to turn on the 'literary mandarins' such as Sutherland who it would seem wish to keep them silent. In response, Richard Charkin, CEO of publisher Macmillan (cited by Cooke 2006) perched himself firmly on the fence, acknowledging that newspaper reviews were more 'credible' and that now 'there are so many words, the impact of any review is diluted', but recognising the existence of a 'clique' and celebrating the fact that web reviews opened up new discussion.

The book blog has provided a space for 'tastemakers' since the mid 1990s (Driscoll 2019) with the bloggers often explicitly collaborating with publishers, festivals and authors to promote works, while at the same time representing a range of 'taste cultures' (283) including detailed and nuanced critique. In her study of reviewing in the digital literary sphere, Murray (2018) explores how reviewing has been cultivated by book retailing websites such as Amazon to use the 'language of cultural connoisseurship and curatorship' (18) for commercial and marketing purposes. Meanwhile, Allington's (2016) comparison of Amazon and professional reviews (discussed in Chapter 4) also challenged assumptions that reviews by ordinary consumers would necessarily be less nuanced or detailed.

Such work demonstrates that, whether or not cultural capital and power is shifting or becoming more evenly distributed, what we can be certain of is that the visible participation of wider groups of people in discussions around the literary is becoming harder to ignore and is provoking renewed debates around notions of literary taste and value. Undoubtedly, social media contributes to the celebrification of authorship and is used by publishers and individual authors to shamelessly sell and promote content. However, alongside new opportunities for users to themselves create and share content, more and more opportunities exist for people to establish themselves as intermediaries or gatekeepers, while just as many others may turn to social media for guidance or access to literary materials that might previously have been impossible to source. Clearly, the roles we have traditionally assigned and compartmentalised in terms of the production, dissemination and reception of the literary are now in constant flux and negotiation. What social media also brings to the fore is how literature can divide as well as draw people together, providing a space for factions and formations to align and realign, and for new markets to emerge that cater for niche tastes and previously marginalised or dispreferred responses.

Afterword

Over the course of the writing of this book, the relationship between literature and social media has become more firmly established, as more and more of us access and engage with literary content via digital devices where we can move seamlessly between reading a text, catching up with the activities of the author of that text, curating our responses and those of others, and keeping track of notifications and trending topics. Moreover, social media plays an intrinsic role in facilitating the crossing of boundaries between genres and media that is so much a feature of contemporary literature.

The writing of the book has also coincided with many significant changes to social media platforms and apps with regards to their affordances and terms of service. When I first started writing about social media, concerns about privacy, covert surveillance of users, and toxicity were beginning to be expressed, but have since become much more widespread. With regards to the field of literature, over the course of the study several high-profile authors, reviewers and book bloggers have either removed their social media profiles completely or taken breaks from social media usage. And in 2019, a 'vicious war' (Benedictus 2019) was reported to have broken out amongst Young Adult authors, some of whom faced death threats and online abuse over perceived transphobia and racism in their work.

For some users, the only option is to turn to some of the alternative platforms that have emerged claiming to offer a more decentralised, less hate filled space. One such alternative is Mastodon, allowing users to create their own 'instances' which they control and moderate and purporting to put social networking 'back in your hands' (www.mastodon. social). However, there has already been some controversy over groups using Mastodon to share overtly racist content (Makuch 2019), demonstrating once again how the idealism that may well motivate the design of these spaces may soon be undermined.

As has been clear from earlier chapters, market forces and political events have meant that platforms and apps that were hugely popular when I started my study have been displaced by newer rivals. Some have disappeared completely, for example Vine, the short-form video hosting service associated with Twitter which was finally wound down in 2017. To some extent replacing it, Tik Tok, a social media video app which started life in China, has become hugely popular with teenagers, one of its key features being that users do not need to set up user groups or start following others to access a seemingly infinite stream of content purporting to reflect their interests and preferences.

With both Mastodon and Tik Tok, therefore, we are beginning to witness shifts away from cultivating ever larger personal networks, towards smaller or more temporary groupings based on niche, random or bespoke tastes and preferences. Also noticeable over the period of this study is the growth of the use of social media platforms for activism and for trying to leverage online networks to fight back against injustices and the attempted silencing or marginalisation of certain communities. For example, Matthews (2019) has discussed the impact of a **woke** sensibility on literature in relation to the audience for contemporary black feminism with reference to Instapoets such as Yrsa Daley-Ward and to multiplatform book clubs such as the Well-Read Black Girl group active on Twitter and Instagram.

The term 'wokenomics' has been coined to refer to the commercial exploitation of the newly awoken political awareness, where companies or brands set out to take advantage of growing momentum or visibility of certain issues or communities. Throughout this study, I have explored the often complex and contradictory relationship between the literary and the commercial, brought into sharp focus on social media and a culture of sharing and connectivity that demands constant rewards and benefits. Alongside the emergence of ever more opportunities for writers to publish and disseminate their work, we now seem to be witnessing a distinct shift towards monetisation of content and complex relations of patronage and dependency developing between those we can no longer simplistically define as content producers or consumers.

One of the key questions arising out of the preceding discussion is the extent to which any of the examples of literary outputs, activities and forms of engagement that I have discussed will stand the test of time. In previous chapters I have argued that forms of literature encountered on or shared by social media display high performativity, relationality and 'nowness'. In addition, literature as it is encountered on social media is often though not exclusively embedded in and amongst other activities, challenging the perception of the literary as some kind of distinct or remote category hermetically sealed off from the everyday world.

Another key question is whether any of the changes or innovations I have made claims for are any different from the long history literature has of readily adapting to new formats and platforms, and of engaging in a dynamic dialogue between old and new. If we accept that they may offer something new or distinctive, the next question which arises in relation to these forms is how we can hope to preserve them to ensure future generations will be able to have some access to the work being produced and some grasp of the environments that produced them. While I have argued that social media raises the visibility not just of new kinds of literary outputs but also how they are accessed, shared and critiqued by users, that visibility may in practice be very short lived.

In a study of the 'Twittering machine' published in 2019, Seymour launches now familiar attacks on social media as addictive and as encouraging hateful trolling and lying. He also reacts negatively to the idea of social media as a nightmarish 'collective writing experiment' (2019: 139) in which we are 'swimming in writing' (23), and constantly either writing ourselves or being written about. However, I would argue that this is not in itself a bad thing, especially where (as discussed in Chapter 4) those participating in the production of this writing contribute to its curation and critique. As my survey of responses to the rise of electronic literature (in Chapter 1) highlighted, new forms of literary output can only thrive where there is a critical infrastructure and poetics that can help us to account for, evaluate and communicate what might give that work value, resonance and meaning. Throughout this study, I have therefore tried to identify new theoretical models and paradigms, for example post-postmodernism or new materialism that might help point the way to such new understandings of the place and purpose of the literary.

What I have also attempted to do in this study is to step outside both abstract theorising and a narrow focus on form, language or technique, to engage with how literary experiments with social media impact on authors, readers and the literary industry in its broadest sense, arguing that social media makes it both possible and in some senses necessary for us to take this 360° approach. For me, it is therefore unthinkable that I should discuss literary outputs on social media without thinking about the responses, processes and affordances that are so crucial to understanding how they are situated, activated and circulated, tagged and archived often by multiple users in a multiplicity of ways, some undoubtedly influenced by age old ways of responding to and evaluating the literary, but some drawing on different sets of dynamics or politics, or the unpredictable and quirky reactions and interpretations of individual users.

One of the unforeseen issues arising from my attempt to map out this new territory is that in addition to the porous boundaries between creators and consumers, producers and users, it has at times been very difficult to determine to what extent the content I am discussing can be said to exist 'on' social media. For example, in my discussion of Twitterature, many of the quotations I have used are taken from websites rather than from social media platforms or apps, while in other cases, content may spread across platforms, websites and 'old' media. To some extent this reflects how what van Dijck and Poell (2013: 1) call social media logic transcends individual platforms and is 'gradually invading all areas of public life', to the point where some of the practices and discourse types they introduce come to seem natural and all pervasive. Nevertheless, just as some readers of this work may take issue with how I define the literary, or how I define authorship, so too *what* I am claiming to discuss in terms of social media may be encountered differently by readers depending on their access to, familiarity with, and usage of the various types of platforms and apps currently available.

I hope to have succeeded in highlighting the kinds of literary activity already existing on, around or with social media, and to have demonstrated the potential for this activity to develop and to provide rich new material for literary and cultural critics. Having spent the last ten years or so immersed in social media worlds, I have increasingly become aware of and attuned to the controversies they provoke, and the fact that my user experience may be very different from others based on my experience and privileges as an academic with the time and training to manage and monitor my accounts. Nevertheless, I find myself continually enlightened and enriched by the conversations and creative experiments social media facilitate, and while I am excited by what the future may hold, I hope that some of the platforms and apps that I currently enjoy using will be around at least for some time yet.

Glossary

Actor Network Theory	approach to social theory associated in particular with Latour (2005) based on examining the infrastructures of shifting networks of relations. Linked to New Materialism in its focus on connections or relations that run *between* the human and nonhuman
Affordances	qualities/features/properties of an object that define its potential uses
Algorithm	a list of steps to follow a problem involving calculation, processing of data, automated tasks
Analytics	processes for drawing insights from raw data/ information sources
App (application)	software program designed for a specific purpose, particularly associated with mobile devices
ARG	alternative reality game
Attention economy	based on the idea of human attention as a resource or commodity (Davenport and Beck 2001)
Beta reader	a term used in fan cultures for an experienced member of a fan community who gives advice to newer members on all aspects of their writing
Bookblog/vlog	discussion/information about books and readings by means of a website or video sharing platform e.g. YouTube
Bookstagram	the creation and sharing of an image relating to books/reading via Instagram
BookTube	subset or community of people posting content relating to books and reading via YouTube
Born digital literature	literature written for and read on a computer screen

Bot	a software application set up to manage automated tasks
Canon	body of works and writers/artists held to be definitive of the highest standards relating to a specific cultural or national history and tradition
Convergence	as defined by Henry Jenkins (2006a) the flow of content across multiple media platforms, cooperation between media industries and the migratory behaviour of audiences
Creepypasta	horror stories shared via the internet/social media based on the idea of copying and pasting text
Crowdfunding	the practice of funding a venture or project by sourcing small contributions from multiple sources
Cultural intermediaries	defined by Matthews and Smith Maguire (2014:1) as 'the taste makers defining what counts as good taste and cool culture in today's marketplace'
Digital humanities	an academic field that applies computational tools and methods (often on a large scale) to the study of traditional humanities subjects
Distant reading	as practised by e.g. Moretti (2013) the opposite of close reading, relying on computational analysis to facilitate the investigation of large collections of texts and the identification of patterns or recurring features across those collections
Distributed narratives	as defined by Walker (2004) narratives emerging from network cultures and relying on the digital that cross media, time, location etc.
Echo chamber	the idea that social media only amplifies and reinforces existing beliefs amongst users, challenged by internet theorist Bruns (2017) for lack of evidence
Fanfiction	stories produced by fans based on characters, plotlines and tropes from pre-existing sources
Fanon	information and accounts and interpretations of fan texts that become accepted and widely distributed by fan communities
Flarf	experimental poetic writing based on the language of internet search engines e.g. Google

Following	the practice of electing to receive content from a social media account
Geotag	adding geographical metadata to media
Gif (Graphics Interchange Format)	image format that supports animation
Hashtag	a word or phrase preceded by the symbol # used across social media platforms for tagging content to make topics discoverable by other users
Hauntology	term coined by Derrida (1994) referring to how the spectre of the past haunts the present, later also used (e.g. by Fisher 2014) in relation to music and popular culture in relation to notions of nostalgia and the weird/eerie hauntings of memory
Hypertext	text that links to other text or documents
Influencer	person or group that has sufficient authority or credibility to allow them to influence behaviour and opinion of significant numbers of other people
Interactive storytelling	narratives that respond to the input of users in some way
Interface	the point at which the user/computer/software interact or communicate with each other
Life writing	the recording of memories and experiences in the form of autobiography, journal, diary, etc.
Like	a way of signalling support for a post on social media, although the precise meaning and significance will vary according to context
Locative media	media often with a strong narrative element which is tied to a particular location often through reference to GPS (global positioning systems) data
Ludic	used in the context of discussion of games to refer to an experience or form of use which may be distinct from narrative (as also in the term ludology)
Meme	image, sound, video, text copied and spread by users
Multimodality	communication which uses multiple modes (aural, visual, textual, spatial)
Netflix	subscription streaming service which allows users to watch tv and film content on multiple devices

Netnography	online research methodology based on ideas and practices from ethnography
New Materialism	interdisciplinary theory (Bennett 2010; Coole and Frost 2010) which seeks a repositioning of the human and challenges essentialist dualisms and divisions e.g. between the human and non-human, active subjects and inert objects/'things'
Nowness	as originally defined by John Fiske (1987) narratives which appear unwritten and 'live' which position the viewer alongside the characters experiencing events
Parasocial	as defined by Horton and Wohl (1956) one-sided relationships especially as formed by media audience members in relation to media figures and celebrities
Paratext	defined by Genette (1997) as the 'threshold to the text', widely used in media and fan studies e.g. to include discussion of marketing and promotional materials in relation to tv or film franchises
Participant observation	observation and participation in activities aimed at developing a detailed and intimate insight into a particular group or phenomenon
Participatory culture	term coined by Henry Jenkins (2006b) to refer particularly to fan and online cultures where creativity and engagement from users and audiences is encouraged and facilitated
Platform	a service, site or method that delivers media content to an audience
Platform studies	field of study which sets out to examine relationship between hardware and software design and creative works produced on computer based systems
Posthumanism	theories which critique traditional notions of the human particularly in relation to technology
Post-postmodern	response to or against postmodernism characterised by some as replacing irony with sincerity
Psychogeography	explorations of the effects of location and place on emotion and behaviour, often through urban wandering. The term was invented by Debord

(1955), and influenced by Baudelaire's concept of the flâneur from the nineteenth century

Read-Write
Lessig's term for a culture where the user can write (or overwrite) content as opposed to a Read-Only culture where the user is a passive consumer

Remediation
as used by Bolter and Grusin (2000) to explore how media constantly borrow, repurpose and refashion other media in the context of debates about the emergence of so-called new media

Retweeting
on Twitter, the act of reposting or forwarding content posted by another user to one's followers

Small stories
as used by Georgakopolou (2007), Page (2010, 2012) and others, particularly to challenge restrictive definitions of narrative that may exclude the ephemeral, inconsequential, fragmentary stories particularly those found within social media contexts

Social networks
in the context of online communication, websites, platforms and applications that allow users to form relations with other users based on shared interests, tastes, activities etc.

Tag
in the context of online spaces and social media a way of notifying others that certain topics, individuals etc. are being mentioned

Technological determinism
the assumption that the emergence of new technologies can be seen as a determining factor in influencing behaviour, thought, social practices etc.

Tweet
a post on Twitter restricted to 280 characters (140 characters until 2017)

Twine
open source tool for creating interactive stories

Uncreative writing
term used by Goldsmith (2011) to examine writing in the digital era and how emerging practices may challenge pre-digital notions of creativity

Web 2.0
term which emerged in the early noughties to refer to a second generation of development of the world wide web facilitating greater user participation and generation of content

Weird Twitter	the practice of experimenting with spelling, punctuation, format to create surreal or absurd writing and effects on Twitter
Woke	increased consciousness or sensitivity to injustice with reference to the idea of becoming alert, waking up from apathy or hopelessness
Wreader/wreading	term originally coined by Landow (1992) to refer to the idea that digital cultures break down the traditional notion of reading and writing as distinct activities

References

Aciman, A. and Rensin, E. (2009) *Twitterature: The World's Greatest Books Retold through Twitter*. London: Penguin Books.

Allington, D. (2016) 'Power to the Reader' or 'Degradation of Literary Taste'? Professional Critics and Amazon Customers as Reviewers of *The Inheritance of Loss*. *Language and Literature*. 25. 3, pp. 254–278.

Andersen, T.R. (2017) Staggered Transmissions: Twitter and the Return of Serialized Literature. *Convergence*. 23. 1, pp. 34–48.

Anderson, B. (1983) *Imagined Communities: Reflections on the Origin and Spread of Nationalism*. London: Verso.

Barekat, H., Barry, R. and Winters, D. (eds) (2017) *The Digital Critic: Literary Culture Online*. New York: OR Books.

Barnet, B. (2018) Hypertext before the Web – or, What the Web Could Have Been. In Brugger, N., Ankerson, M.S. and Milligan, I. (eds) *SAGE Handbook of Web History*. London: Sage, pp. 215–226.

Barry, (2018) A Media of One's Own: The Future of Criticism, in Retrospect. In Barekat, H., Barry, R. and Winters, D. (eds) *The Digital Critic: Literary Culture Online*. New York: OR Books, pp. 68–78.

Barth, J. (1984[1967]) The Literature of Exhaustion. *The Friday Book: Essays and Other Non-Fiction*. Baltimore: Johns Hopkins University Press, pp. 62–76.

Bartholomew, J. (2015) The Awful Rise of 'Virtue Signalling'. *The Spectator*. 18 April. Accessed 13 August 2019 at: https://www.spectator.co.uk/2015/04/ha ting-the-daily-mail-is-a-substitute-for-doing-good/.

Batard, P. (2007) *How To Talk About Books You Haven't Read*. New York: Bloomsbury.

Bath, J., Arbucke, A., Crompton, C., Christie, A., Siemens, R and the INKE Research Group (2018) Futures of the Book. In Sayers, J. (ed.) *The Routledge Companion to Media Studies and Digital Humanities*. London: Routledge, pp. 336–344.

Baym, N., Burgess, J.Cunningham, S., Craig, D., Helmond, A., Bucher, T.John, N. and Nissenbaum, A. (2016) Platform Studies: The Rules of Engagement. *AoIR*

2016. Accessed 29 January 2019 at: https://spir.aoir.org/index.php/spir/article/view/1236.

Beaumont, M. (2000) *e.* London: Harper Collins.

Bell, A., Ensslin, A. and Rustad, H.K. (eds) (2014) *Analysing Digital Fiction.* London: Routledge.

Benedictus, L. (2019) Torn Apart: The Vicious War over Young Adult Books. *The Guardian,* 15 June. Accessed 2 August 2019 at: https://www.theguardian.com/books/2019/jun/15/torn-apart-the-vicious-war-over-young-adult-books?cMP=Share_iOSApp_Other.

Benjamin, W. (1999[1955]) Unpacking my Library. In *Illuminations.* London: Pimlico, pp. 61–69.

Bennett, J. (2010) *Vibrant Matter: A Political Ecology of Things.* Durham, NC: Duke University Press.

Bennett, T. and Woollacott, J. (1987) *Bond and Beyond: The Political Career of a Popular Hero.* Basingstoke: Macmillan.

Bergonzi, B. (1986) *The Myth of Modernism and Twentieth Century Literature.* New York: St Martin's Press.

Bhandara, N. (2017) 18 'Terribly Tiny Tales' Highlight Some of India's Most Pressing Problems. *Homegrown.* 4 March. Accessed 13 August 2019 at: https://homegrown.co.in/article/42022/18-terribly-tiny-tales-highlight-some-of-indias-most-pressing-problems.

Bhaskar, M. (2016) *Curation: the Power of Selection in a World of Excess.* London: Piatkus.

Bilston, B. (2016) *You Took the Last Bus Home.* London: Unbound.

Birkerts, S. (1994) *The Gutenberg Elegies: The Fate of Reading in an Electronic Age.* New York: Fawcett Columbine.

Bode, K. (2012) *Reading by Numbers: Recalibrating the Literary Field.* London: Anthem Press.

Bolat, E. and Gilani, P. (2018) Instagram Influencers: When a Special Relationship with Fans Turns Dark. *The Conversation.* 7 August. Accessed 29 January 2019 at: https://theconversation.com/instagram-influencers-when-a-special-relationship-with-fans-turns-dark-100543.

Bold, M.R. (2016) The Return of the Social Author: Negotiating Authority and Influence on Wattpad. *Convergence.* 24. 2, pp. 117–136.

Bolter, J. (2001) *Writing Space: Computers, Hypertext, and the Remediation of Print.* Cambridge, MA: MIT Press.

Bolter, J. and Grusin, R. (2000) *Remediation: Understanding New Media.* Cambridge, MA: MIT Press.

Bouchardon, S. (2018) Mind the Gap! 10 Gaps for Digital Literature. Accessed 29 January 2019 at: http://www.utc.fr/~bouchard/Bouchardon-ELO18-English.pdf

Bourdieu, P. (1983) The Field of Cultural Production, or: The Economic World Reversed. *Poetics.* 12. 4–5, pp. 311–356.

Bourdieu, P. (1993) *The Field of Cultural Production.* Cambridge: Polity Press.

Braun, R. and Spiers, E. (2016) Introduction: Re-viewing Literary Celebrity. *Celebrity Studies.* 7. 4. pp. 449–456.

Brown, J. (2018) The New York Public Library is Turning Classics into Instagram Stories. *Gizmodo.* 22 August. Accessed 13 August 2019 at: https://gizm odo.com/the-new-york-public-library-is-turning-classics-into-in-1828516803.

Bruns, A. (2017) Echo Chamber? What Echo Chamber? Reviewing the Evidence. In *6th Biennial Future of Journalism Conference*, 14–15 September. Accessed 12 August 2019 at: https://eprints.qut.edu.au/113937/.

Bucur, M. (2017) *Gendering Modernism: A Historical Reappraisal of the Canon.* London: Bloomsbury.

Burgess, J. (2006) Hearing Ordinary Voices: Cultural Studies, Vernacular Creativity and Digital Storytelling. *Continuum.* 20. 2, pp. 201–214.

Burgess, J., Marwick, A. and Poell, T. (2017) *The Sage Handbook of Social Media.* London: Sage.

Byager, L. (2018) Roll your Eyes all you Like, but Instagram Poets are Redefining the Genre for Millennials. *Mashable UK.* 19 October. Accessed 29 January 2019 at: https://mashable.com/article/instagram-poetry-democratise-genre/?europe=true.

Caliandro, A. and Gandini, A. (2017) *Qualitative Research in Digital Environments.* London: Routledge.

Carlson, B. and Frazer, R. (2018) *Social Media Mob: Being Indigenous Online.* Macquarie University. Accessed 29 January 2019 at: https://research-managem ent.mq.edu.au/ws/portalfiles/portal/85013179/MQU_SocialMediaMob_report_ Carlson_Frazer.pdf.

Carpenter, J.R. (2018) Six Questions. *Iota: Data.* Accessed 29 January 2019 at: https://static1.squarespace.com/static/557afa73e4b03c2094a2fdc7/t/5c125a2a70a 6ad32a0d3d904/1544706602840/IOTA-DATA_CarpenterChanSolo.pdf.

Carr, N. (2010) *The Shallows: How the Internet is Changing the Way We Think, Read and Remember.* London: Atlantic.

Charles, R. (2018) Goodreads Choice Awards: An Annual Reminder that Critics and Readers Don't Often Agree. *The Washington Post.* December 4. Accessed 20 November 2019 at: https://www.washingtonpost.com/entertainment/books/ goodreads-choice-awards-an-annual-reminder-that-critics-and-readers-dont-of ten-agree/2018/12/03/0ce76a26-f6f4-11e8-8c9a-860ce2a8148f_story.html.

Chess, S. and Newsom, E. (2015) *Folklore, Horror Stories, and The Slender Man: The Development of an Internet Mythology.* New York: Palgrave Pivot.

Chun, W.H.K. (2016) *Updating to Remain the Same: Habitual New Media.* Cambridge, MA: MIT Press.

Clarke, A. (2015) *Follow Me.* London: Avon.

Colclough, S. (2011) Representing Reading Spaces. In Crone, R. and Towheed, S. (eds) *The History of Reading, Volume 3.* Basingstoke: Palgrave Macmillan, pp. 99–114.

Cole, T. (n.d) Small Fates. Accessed 23 February 2016 at: www.tejucole.com/sma llfates.

Coleman, M. (2018) How Book Twitter has Turned Writers into Extroverts. *Book Riot.* 10 October. Accessed 29 January 2019 at: https://bookriot.com/ 2018/10/10/how-book-twitter-has-turned-writers-into-extroverts/.

Collins, J. (2010) *Bring on the Books for Everybody: How Literary Culture Became Popular Culture.* Durham, NC: Duke University Press.

Connolly, H. (2018) Is Social Media Influencing Book Cover Design? *The Guardian*. 28 August. Accessed 29 January 2019 at: https://www.theguardian.com/books/2018/aug/28/is-social-media-influencing-book-cover-design.

Cooke, R. (2006) Deliver Us from these Latter-day Pooters. *The Guardian*. 26 November. Accessed 29 January 2019 at: https://www.theguardian.com/arta nddesign/2006/nov/26/art1.

Coole, D.H. and Frost, S. (2010) *New Materialisms: Ontology, Agency, and Politics*. Durham, NC: Duke University Press.

Coover, R. (1992) The End of Books. *The New York Times*. 21 June. Accessed 29 January 2019 at: http://movies2.nytimes.com/books/98/09/27/specials/coover-end.html.

Couldry, N. (2006) *Listening Beyond the Echoes: Media, Ethics, and Agency in an Uncertain World*. London: Routledge.

Couldry, N. (2008) Actor Network Theory and Media: Do They Connect and On What Terms. In Hepp, A., Krotz, F., Moores, S. and Winter, C. (eds) *Connectivity, Networks and Flows: Conceptualizing Contemporary Communications*. Cresskill, NJ: Hampton Press, pp. 93–110.

Couldry, N. and Mejias, U.A. (2018) Data Colonialism: Rethinking Big Data's Relation to the Contemporary Subject. *Television and New Media*. Accessed 29 January 2019 at: https://journals.sagepub.com/doi/10.1177/1527476418796632.

Coupland, D. (1996) *Microserfs*. New York: Harper Perennial.

Cousins, H. and Ramone, J. (eds) (2011) *The Richard and Judy Book Club Reader*. London: Ashgate.

Cox, C. (2018) *she must be mad*. London: Harper Collins.

Crouch, I. (2014) The Great American Twitter Novel. *The New Yorker*. 23 July. Accessed 29 January 2019 at: https://www.newyorker.com/books/page-turner/great-american-twitter-novel.

Danielewski, M.Z. (2000) *House of Leaves*. New York: Pantheon.

Davenport, T.H. and Beck, J.C. (2001) *The Attention Economy: Understanding the New Currency of Business*. Cambridge, MA: Harvard Business Press.

Davies, R. (2017) Collaborative Production and the Transformation of Publishing: The Case of Wattpad. In Graham, J. and Gandini, A. (eds) *Collaborative Production in the Creative Industries*. London: University of Westminster Press, pp. 51–67.

Debord, G. (1955) Introduction a une critique de la géographie urbaine. *Les Lévres nues*. No.6.

De León, C. (2019) Wattpad, the Storytelling App, Will Launch a Publishing Division. *The New York Times*. 24 January. Accessed 29 January 2019 at: https://www.nytimes.com/2019/01/24/books/wattpad-books-publishing-division.html.

Dena, C. (2009) Transmedia Practice: Theorising the Practice of Expressing a Fictional World across Distinct Media and Environments. PhD thesis. University of Sydney.

Derrida, J. (1994) *Spectres of Marx*. Transl. by P. Kamuf. London: Routledge.

Dix, H. (2017) *The Late-Career Novelist*. London: Bloomsbury.

Docherty, T. (2014) The Paratext's the Thing. *The Chronicle of Higher Education*. 6 January. Accessed 29 January 2019 at: https://www.chronicle.com/article/The-Paratexts-the-Thing/143761.

Dockray, H. (2019) Welcome to 'Deep Bookstagram', where Dark, Book-Based Comedy Thrives. *Mashable.* 10 June. Accessed 15 July 2019 at: https://masha ble.com/article/best-weird-bookstagram/?europe=true.

Dourish, P. and Cruz, E.G. (2018) Datafication and Data Fiction: Narrating Data and Narrating with Data. *Big Data and Society.* 5. 2. Accessed 29 January 2019 at: https://journals.sagepub.com/doi/10.1177/2053951718784083.

Driscoll, B. (2014) *The New Literary Middlebrow: Tastemakers and Reading in the Twenty-First Century.* Basingstoke: Palgrave Macmillan.

Driscoll, B. (2015) Sentiment Analysis and the Literary Festival Audience. *Continuum.* 29. 6, pp. 861–873.

Driscoll, B. (2019) Book Blogs as Tastemakers. *Participations.* 16. 1, pp. 280–305.

Driscoll, B. and Rehberg Sedo, D. (2019) Faraway, So Close: Seeing the Intimacy in Goodreads Reviews. *Qualitative Inquiry.* 25. 3, pp. 248–259.

Eberly, R. (2000) *Citizen Critics: Literary Public Spheres.* Chicago: University of Illinois Press.

Edwards, M. and Voss, L. (2013) *Forward Slash.* London: Harper Collins.

Egan, J. (2011) *A Visit from the Goon Squad.* London: Corsair.

Egan, J. (2012) *Black Box.* London: Corsair.

Eggers, D. (2013) *The Circle.* London: Penguin.

English, J.F. (2005) *The Economy of Prestige.* Cambridge, MA: Harvard University Press.

Ensslin, A. (2007) *Canonizing Hypertext.* London: Continuum.

Ensslin, A. (2014) *Literary Gaming.* Cambridge, MA: MIT Press.

Escoria, J. (2015) Mira Gonzalez and Tao Lin's Selected Tweets is Deeper Than It Seems. *Fader.* 8 June. Accessed 29 January 2019 at: https://www.thefader. com/2015/06/08/mira-gonzalez-tao-lin-twitter-interview-with-juliet-escoria.

Feng, J. (2012) Have Mouse, Will Travel: Consuming and Creating Chinese Popular Literature on the Web. In Lang, A. *From Codex to Hypertext: Reading at the Turn of the Twenty-First Century.* Amherst: University of Massachusetts Press, pp. 48–67.

Ferguson, D. (2019a) Poetry Sales Soar as Political Millennials Search for Clarity. *The Guardian.* 21 January. Accessed 29 January 2019 at: https://www.theguardian.com/ books/2019/jan/21/poetry-sales-soar-as-political-millennials-search-for-clarity.

Ferguson, D. (2019b) 'Keats is dead...': How Young Women Are Changing the Rules of Poetry. *The Guardian.* 26 January. Accessed 29 January 2019 at: https:// www.theguardian.com/books/2019/jan/26/new-generation-young-women-poets.

Fielding, H. (1996) *Bridget Jones's Diary.* London: Picador.

Fielding, H. (2013) *Mad About the Boy.* London: Jonathan Cape.

Finn, E. (2012) New Literary Cultures. In Lang, A. (ed.) *From Codex to Hypertext: Reading at the Turn of the Twenty-First Century.* Amherst: University of Massachusetts Press, pp. 177–202.

Fisher, M. (2014) *Ghosts of My Life: Writings on Depression, Hauntology and Lost Futures.* Alresford: Zero Books.

Fiske, J. (1987) *Television Culture.* London: Routledge.

Fitzpatrick, K. (2006) *The Anxiety of Obsolescence: The American Novel in the Age of Television.* Nashville: Vanderbilt University Press.

Flatt, M. (2017) Last Seen Online Offers a 'New Genre' for the WhatsApp Generation. *The Bookseller.* 27 January. Accessed 29 January 2019 at: https://www.thebookseller.com/futurebook/last-seen-online-offers-new-genre-whats-app-generation-475751.

Flint, K. (2011) Books in Photographs. In Crone, R. and Towheed, S. (eds) *The History of Reading, Volume 3.* Basingstoke: Palgrave Macmillan, pp. 156–173.

Flood, A. (2016) Emojis Worth a Thousand Words: Classic Novels Retold in Smileys. *The Guardian.* 17 August. Accessed 5 August 2019 at: https://www.theguardian.com/books/booksblog/2016/aug/17/emojis-worth-a-thousand-words-classic-novels-retold-in-smileys-kyle-maclachlan-dune.

Flood, A. and Cain, S. (2018) Poetry World Split over Polemic Attacking 'Amateur' Work by 'Young Female Poets'. *The Guardian.* 23 January. Accessed 29 January 2019 at: https://www.theguardian.com/books/2018/jan/23/poetry-world-split-over-polemic-attacking-amateur-work-by-young-female-poets.

Flood, A. (2019) Why Should Authors Read Your Bad Reviews? *The Guardian.* 1 July. Accessed 16 July 2019 at: https://www.theguardian.com/books/booksblog/2019/jul/01/why-should-authors-read-your-bad-reviews?CMP=Share_iOSApp_Other.

Flores, L. (2018) Third Generation Electronic Literature. Accessed 13 August 2019 at: http://leonardoflores.net/blog/presentations-2/lecture-third-generation-electronic-literature/.

Florini, S. (2013) Tweets, Tweeps, and Signifyin': Communication and Cultural Performance on 'Black Twitter'. *Television and New Media.* 15. 3. Accessed 29 January 2019 at: https://journals.sagepub.com/doi/abs/10.1177/1527476413480247?journalCode=tvna.

Foer, J.S. (2005) *Extremely Loud and Incredibly Close.* London: Penguin Books.

Foucault, M. (1991[1969]) What is an Author? In P. Rabinow (ed.) *The Foucault Reader.* London: Penguin, pp. 101–120.

Franklin, R. (2014) Can You Write a Novel on Twitter? *Foreign Policy.* 28 November. Accessed 29 January 2019 at: http://foreignpolicy.com/2014/11/28/can-you-write-a-novel-on-twitter.

Freeman-Powell, S. (2019) The Rock Stars of Poetry Explain why the Art is in Demand. Accessed 29 January 2019 at: https://www.bbc.co.uk/news/entertainment-arts-47005108.

Fuchs, C. (2013) *Social Media: A Critical Introduction.* London: Sage.

Fuller, D. and Rehberg Sedo, D. (2013) *Reading Beyond the Book.* London: Routledge.

Fülöp, E. (2019) Digital Authorship and Social Media: French Digital Authors' Attitudes towards Facebook. *French Cultural Studies.* 30. 2, pp. 121–137.

Gallucci, N. (2018) In a World of e-readers, Book Instagram Wants you to Pick Up a Hardcover. *MashableUK.* 11 September. Accessed 29 January 2019 at: https://mashable.com/article/best-instagram-accounts-for-book-lovers/?europe=true.

Gee, J.P. (2004) *Situated Language and Learning.* London: Routledge.

Gee, J.P. and Hayes, E. (2012) Nurturing Affinity Spaces and Game-Based Learning. In Steinkuehler, C., Squire, K. and Barab, S. (eds) *Games, Learning, and Society: Learning and Meaning in the Digital Age*. Cambridge: Cambridge University Press, pp. 129–153.

Geffen, S. (n.d) #Hashtag Boost: The Internet Poetics of Steve Roggenbuck. *Impose*. Accessed 20 November 2019 at: https://www.imposemagazine.com/fea tures/hashtag-boost-steve-roggenbuck.

Genette, G. (1997) *Paratexts: Thresholds of Interpretation*. Transl. by Jane E. Lewin. Cambridge: Cambridge University Press.

Georgakopolou, A. (2007) *Small Stories, Interaction and Identities*. Amsterdam: John Benjamins Publishing Company.

Gerken, T. (2018) Tsundoku: The Art of Buying Books and Never Reading Them. Accessed 19 November 2019 at: https://www.bbc.co.uk/news/ world-44981013.

Gibbons, A. (2012) *Multimodality, Cognition, and Experimental Literature*. London: Routledge.

Gibbs, M., Meese, J., Arnold, M., Nansen, B. and Carter, M. (2015) #Funeral and Instagram: Death, Social Media and Platform Vernacular. *Information, Communication & Society*. 18. 3, pp. 255–268.

Goggin, G. and Hamilton, C. (2014) Narrative Fiction and Mobile Media after the Text-Message Novel. In Farman, J. (ed.) *The Mobile Story*. Abingdon: Routledge, pp. 223–237.

Goldsmith, K. (2011) *Uncreative Writing: Managing Language in the Digital Age*. New York: Columbia University Press.

Goldsmith, K. (2014) If Walt Whitman Vlogged. *The New Yorker*. 7 May. Accessed 29 January 2019 at: https://www.newyorker.com/books/page-turner/ if-walt-whitman-vlogged.

Goody, A. (2011) *Technology, Literature and Culture*. Cambridge: Polity Press.

Goodyear, D. (2008) I ♥ Novels. *The New Yorker*. 22 December. Accessed 29 January 2019 at: https://www.newyorker.com/magazine/2008/12/22/i-love-novels.

Gray, J. (2010) *Show Sold Separately: Promos, Spoilers, and Other Media Paratexts*. New York: New York University Press.

Green, H. (2018) *An Absolutely Remarkable Thing*. London: Trapeze.

Gwynne, K. (2015) 10 Authors who Excel on the Internet. *The Guardian*. 11 May. Accessed 29 January 2019 at: https://www.theguardian.com/books/2015/may/11/ 10-authors-who-excel-on-the-internet.

Hale, K. (2014) 'Am I being catfished?' An Author Confronts her Number One Online Critic. *The Guardian*. 18 October. Accessed 16 January 2019 at: https://www. theguardian.com/books/2014/oct/18/am-i-being-catfished-an-author-confronts-her- number-one-online-critic.

Hammond, A. (2016) *Literature in the Digital Age*. Cambridge: Cambridge University Press.

Harris, J. (2015) A Writer's Manifesto. Manchester Literary Festival. Accessed 20 November 2019 at: http://www.manchesterliteraturefestival.co.uk/pages/joanne-ha rris—a-writers-manifesto-37061.

Hayles, N.K. (2007) Hyper and Deep Attention: The Generational Divide in Cognitive Modes. *Profession*, pp. 187–199.

Hayles, N.K. (2008) *Electronic Literature: New Horizons for the Literary*. Notre Dame: Notre Dame University Press.

Heasley, G. (2014) *Don't Call Me Baby*. New York: Harper Teen.

Hilliard, C. (2006) *To Exercise Our Talents: The Democratization of Writing in Britain*. Cambridge, MA: Harvard University Press.

Hills, M. (2018) An Extended Foreword: From Fan Doxa to Toxic Fan Practices? *Participations*. 15. 1, pp. 105–126.

Holmes, J. (2013) Twitter Storytelling as a New Literacy Practice. *Selected Papers of Internet Research*. 14. 0. Accessed 29 January 2019 at: https://spir. aoir.org/index.php/spir/article/view/782.

Hope, C. (2018) Tory Rebels Set Up WhatsApp Plot to Thwart Theresa May's Brexit Plan. *The Telegraph*. 15 July. Accessed 29 January 2019 at: https:// www.telegraph.co.uk/politics/2018/07/15/eurosceptic-tory-mps-set-party-withi n-party-whipping-operation/.

Horton, D. and Wohl, R.R. (1956) Mass Communication and Para-Social Interaction. *Journal of Psychiatry*. 19. 3. pp. 215–229.

Hungerford, A. (2016) *Making Literature Now*. Stanford, CA: Stanford University Press.

Jackson, S. (1995) *Patchwork Girl*. Watertown, MA: Eastgate Systems.

Jagoda, P. (2016) *Network Aesthetics*. Chicago, IL: The University of Chicago Press.

Jenkins, H. (1992) *Textual Poachers: Television Fans and Participatory Culture*. London: Routledge.

Jenkins, H. (2006a) *Convergence Culture: Where Old and New Media Collide*. New York: New York University Press.

Jenkins, H. (2006b) *Fans, Bloggers, and Gamers: Exploring Participatory Culture*. New York: New York University Press.

Jenkins, H. (2007) Transmedia Storytelling 101. Accessed 29 January 2019 at: http://henryjenkins.org/blog/2007/03/transmedia_storytelling_101.html.

Jenkins, H. (2009) *Confronting the Challenges of Participatory Culture*. Cambridge, MA: MIT Press.

Jenkins, H., Ford, S. and Green, J. (2013) *Spreadable Media: Value and Meaning in a Networked Culture*. New York: New York University Press.

Jenkins, H. and Kelley, W. (2013) *Reading in a Participatory Culture*. New York: Teachers College Press.

John, N. (2016) *The Age of Sharing*. Cambridge: Polity Press.

Jones, B. (2014) Fifty Shades of Exploitation: Fan Labor and Fifty Shades of Grey. *Transformative Works and Cultures*. 15. Accessed 29 January 2019 at: https:// journal.transformativeworks.org/index.php/twc/article/view/501/422.

Jones, H.A. (2016) New Media Producing New Labor: Pinterest, Yearning and Self-Surveillance. *Critical Studies in Media Communication*. 33. 4, pp. 352–365.

Kelley, B. (2016) Toward a Goodwill Ethics of Online Research Methods. *Transformative Works and Cultures*. 22. Accessed 29 January 2019 at: https:// journal.transformativeworks.org/index.php/twc/article/view/891/666.

Kember, S. and Zylinska, J. (2012) *Life After New Media*. Cambridge, MA: MIT Press.

Kirschenbaum, M. (2015) What is an @uthor? *Los Angeles Review of Books*. 6 February. Accessed 29 January 2019 at: https://lareviewofbooks.org/article/uthor#!.

Kirschenbaum, M. (2016) *Track Changes: A Literary History of Word Processing*. Cambridge, MA: Harvard University Press.

Kosmatopoulous, E. (2013) SIRI & Me. Accessed 19 November 2019 at: https://www.esmeraldakosmatopoulos.com/siri-me.

Koul, S. (2019) Kathleen Hale Came For Her Goodreads Critic. Then the Internet Came for Her. *BuzzFeedNews*. 20 June. Accessed 16 July 2019 at: https://www.buzzfeednews.com/article/scaachikoul/kathleen-hale-goodreads-catfish-crazy-stalker.

Kozel, S. (2014) Dancing with Twitter: Mobile Narratives Become Physical Scores. In Farman, J. (ed.) *The Mobile Story: Narrative Practices with Locative Technologies*. London: Routledge, pp. 79–94.

Kozinets, R. (2010) *Netnography: Doing Ethnographic Research Online*. London: Sage.

Landow, G. (1992) *Hypertext: The Convergence of Contemporary Critical Theory and Technology*. Baltimore: Johns Hopkins University Press.

Lanier, J. (2018) *Ten Arguments for Deleting Your Social Media Accounts Right Now*. London: Bodley Head.

Laquintano, T. (2016) *Mass Authorship and the Rise of Self-Publishing*. Iowa City: University of Iowa Press.

Latour, B. (2005) *Reassembling the Social*. Oxford: Oxford University Press.

Lea, R. (2006) The Blogosphere Takes on the Power of the Press. *The Guardian*. 20 November. Accessed 29 January 2019 at: https://www.theguardian.com/books/booksblog/2006/nov/20/theblogospheretakesonthep.

Lehner, S. (2014) Marketing to Millennials: Using Snapchat and Tinder to Promote your TV Show. *Miptrends*. 5 August. Accessed 29 January 2019 at: http://mipblog.com/2014/08/marketing-millennials-using-snapchat-tinder-promote-tv-show/#.VIGKsouOdsj.

Lessig, L. (2008) *Remix: Making Art and Commerce Thrive in the Hybrid Economy*. London: Bloomsbury.

Levey, N. (2016) Post-Press Literature: Self-Published Authors in the Literary Field. *Post 45*. Accessed 29 January 2019 at: http://post45.research.yale.edu/2016/02/post-press-literature-self-published-authors-in-the-literary-field-3/.

Lévy, P. (1997) *Collective Intelligence: Mankind's Emerging World in Cyberspace*. New York: Perseus Books.

Lim, W.M. (2016) Understanding the Selfie Phenomenon. *European Journal of Marketing*. 50.9/10, pp. 1773–1788.

Lin, T. (2013) *Taipei*. Edinburgh: Canongate.

Livingstone, S. (2018) Audiences in an Age of Datafication: Critical Questions for Media Research. *Television and New Media*. 20. 2. Accessed 29 January 2019 at: https://journals.sagepub.com/doi/full/10.1177/1527476418811118.

Lochrie, M. and Coulton, P. (2012) The Role of Smartphones in Mass Participation TV. In *Proceedings of EuroITV 2012 10th European Interactive TV Conference*.

Lodge, D. (1984) *Small World*. Harmondsworth: Penguin Books.

Lovell, N. (2019) *The Pyramid of Game Design*. Boca Raton, FL: CRC Press.

Lovink, G. and Rasch, M. (2013) *Unlike Us Reader: Social Media Monopolies and their Alternatives*. Amsterdam: Institute of Network Cultures.

Madrigal, A. (2018) The Case Against Retweets. *The Atlantic*. April. Accessed 29 January 2019 at: https://www.theatlantic.com/magazine/archive/2018/04/the-case-against-retweets/554078/.

Madrigal, A. (2019) The 'Platform' Excuse is Dying. *The Atlantic*. 11 June. Accessed 16 July 2019 at: https://www.theatlantic.com/technology/archive/2019/06/facebook-and-youtubes-platform-excuse-dying/591466/.

Mäkelä, M. (2019) Literary Facebook Narratology: Experientiality, Simultaneity, Tellability. *Partial Answers*. 17. 1, pp. 159–182.

Makuch, B. (2019) The Nazi-Free Alternative to Twitter is Now Home to the Biggest Far Right Social Network. Accessed 2 August 2019 at: https://www.vice.com/en_us/article/mb8y3x/the-nazi-free-alternative-to-twitter-is-now-home-to-the-biggest-far-right-social-network?utm_campaign=sharebutton.

Malloy, J. (1991) 'Uncle Roger', an Online Narrabase. *Leonardo*. 24. 2.

Malloy, J. (2016) *Social Media Archeology and Poetics*. Cambridge, MA: MIT Press.

Mangen, A. and van der Weel, A. (2015) Why Don't We Read Hypertext Novels? *Convergence*. 23. 2, pp. 166–181.

Manovich, L. (2001) *The Language of New Media*. Cambridge MA: MIT Press.

Marber, P. (1997) *Closer*. London: Methuen.

Margini, M. (2017) 'Hamlet on the Holodeck,' Twenty Years Later. *The New Yorker*. 30 August. Accessed 29 January 2019 at: https://www.newyorker.com/books/second-read/hamlet-on-the-holodeck-twenty-years-later.

Margolin, U. (1999) Of What is Past, Is Passing, or to Come: Temporality, Aspectuality, Modality, and the Nature of Literary Narrative. In Herman, D. (ed.) *Narratologies*. Columbus: Ohio State University Press, pp. 142–166.

Marino, M.C. and Wittig, R. (2015) *I Work for the Web*. Accessed 19 November 2019 at: http://robwit.net/iwfw/.

Marsden, S. (2018) 'I didn't know you could read': Questioning the Legitimacy of Kim Kardashian-West's Status as a Cultural and Literary Intermediary. *Logos*. 29. 2–3, pp. 64–79.

Marsden, S. and Branagh-Miscampbell, M. (2019) 'Eating, Sleeping, Breathing, Reading': The Zoella Book Club and the Young Woman Reader in the 21st Century. *Participations*. 16. 1. pp. 412–440.

Martell, F. (2015) *L'Écrivain 'social': La condition d'écrivain à l'âge numérique*. Accessed 16 July 2019 at: https://gallery.mailchimp.com/1e809b25a8e0be448d87c3d87/files/ressource_fichier_fr_condition_a_crivain_monde_num a_rique_rapport_2015_11_09_ok.pdf.

Martens, M. (2016) *Publishers, Readers, and Digital Engagement: Participatory Forums and Young Adult Publishing*. London: Palgrave Macmillan.

Marwick, A. (2013) *Status Update: Celebrity, Publicity, and Branding in the Social Media Age*. New Haven: Yale University Press.

Matthews, J. and Smith Maguire, J. (eds) (2014) *The Cultural Intermediaries Reader*. London: Sage.

Matthews, K. (2019) 'Woke' and Reading: Social Media, Reception, and Contemporary Black Feminism. *Participations*. 16. 1, pp. 390–411.

May, K. (2018) *The Whitstable High Tide Swimming Club*. London: Trapeze.

McCracken, E. (2013) Expanding Genette's Epitext/Peritext Model for Transitional Electronic Literature. *Narrative*. 21. 1, pp. 105–124.

McDougall, A.C. (2019) What is Cyber-Consciousness? Digital Intermediation between Consciousness and Computer through Postmodern Tension in Tao Lin's Taipei. *C21 Literature*. 7. 1, pp. 1–27.

McNulty, T. (2018) Physical Books, Digital Lives. *Public Books*. 10 November. Accessed 29 January 2019 at: https://www.publicbooks.org/physical-books-digital-lives/.

McRobbie, A. (2016) *Be Creative: Making a Living in the New Culture Industries*. Cambridge: Polity Press.

Mezreich, B. (2009) *The Accidental Billionaires*. New York: Doubleday.

Milgrim, D. (2012) *Siri & Me: A Modern Love Story*. London: Penguin.

Miller, L. (1998) www.claptrap.com. *The New York Times*. 15 March. Accessed 29 January 2019 at: https://archive.nytimes.com/www.nytimes.com/books/98/03/15/bookend/bookend.html?_r=1&oref=slogin.

Mitchell, D. (2014) *The Bone Clocks*. London: Sceptre.

Mittell, J. (2015) *Complex TV: The Poetics of Contemporary Television Storytelling*. New York: New York University Press.

Moran, C. and Hawisher, G.E. (1998) The Rhetorics and Languages of Electronic Mail. In Snyder, I. (ed.) *Page to Screen: Taking Literacy into the Electronic Era*. London: Routledge, pp. 80–101.

Moretti, F. (2013) *Distant Reading*. London: Verso.

Morris, J.W. and Murray, S. (2018) *Appified: Culture in the Age of Apps*. Ann Arbor: University of Michigan Press.

Munteanu, D.G. (2017) Improbably Curators: Analysing Nostalgia, Authorship and Audience on Tumblr Microblogs. In Graham, J. and Gandini, A. (eds) *Collaborative Production in the Creative Industries*. London: University of Westminster Press, pp. 125–156.

Murray, J.H. (1997) *Hamlet on the Holodeck: The Future of Narrative in Cyberspace*. Cambridge MA: MIT Press.

Murray, S. (2012) *The Adaptation Industry*. London: Routledge.

Murray, S. (2018) *The Digital Literary Sphere: Reading, Writing, and Selling Books in the Internet Era*. Baltimore: Johns Hopkins University Press.

Myers, G. (2016) Everyday Oracles: Authors on Twitter. *Celebrity Studies*. 7. 4, pp. 476–492.

Nakamura, L. (2013) 'Words with Friends': Socially Networked Reading on Goodreads. *PMLA*. 128. 1, pp. 238–243.

Nelles, W. (2012) Microfiction: What Makes a Very Short Story Very Short? *Narrative.* 20. 1, pp. 87–104.

Newton, C. (2018) The End of Instagram as We Know It Is Here. *The Verge.* 25 September. Accessed 18 November 2019 at: https://www.theverge.com/2018/9/25/17903556/instagram-founders-quit-kevin-systrom-mike-krieger-facebook.

Norrick-Rühl, C. (2016) (Furniture) Books and Book Furniture as Markers of Authority. *txt magazine.* 2, pp. 2–8.

O'Connell, M. (2018) The Deliberate Awfulness of Social Media. *The New Yorker.* 18 September. Accessed 29 January 2019 at: https://www.newyorker.com/books/under-review/the-deliberate-awfulness-of-social-media.

Ondrak, J. (2018) Spectres des Monstres: Post-postmodernisms, Hauntology and Creepypasta Narratives as Digital Fiction. *Horror Studies.* 9. 2, pp. 161–178.

Page, R. (2010) Re-examining Narrativity: Small Stories in Status Updates. *Text & Talk.* 30. 4, pp. 423–444.

Page, R. (2011) Blogging on the Body: Gender and Narrative. In Page, R. and Thomas, B. (eds) *New Narratives: Stories and Storytelling in the Digital Age.* Lincoln, NE: University of Nebraska Press.

Page, R. (2012) *Stories and Social Media.* London: Routledge.

Page, R. (2017) Ethics Revisited: Rights, Responsibilities and Relationships in Online Research. *Applied Linguistics Review.* 8. 2–3, pp. 315–320.

Page, R. and Thomas, B. (2011) *New Narratives: Stories and Storytelling in the Digital Age.* Lincoln, NE: University of Nebraska Press.

Papacharissi, Z. (2013) A Networked Self: Identity, Performance and Sociability on Social Network Sites. In Lee, F.L.F., Leung, L., Qiu, L. and Chu, D.S.C. (eds) *Frontiers in New Media Research.* London: Routledge, pp. 207–221.

Papacharissi, Z. and Easton, E. (2013) In the Habitus of the New: Structure, Agency, and the Social Media Habitus. In Hartley, J., Burgess, J. and Bruns, A. (eds) *A Companion to New Media Dynamics.* Oxford: Blackwell, pp. 167–184.

Parody, C. (2011) Franchising/Adaptation. *Adaptation.* 4. 2, pp. 210–218.

Patti, E. (2016) From Text to Screen/From Screen to Text. Collaborative Narratives in Twenty-first Century Italian Fiction: The Wu Ming Case. *Journal of Romance Studies.* 16. 1, pp. 39–61.

Pearce, M. (2011) Death by Twitter. *The New Inquiry.* 13 October. Accessed 29 January 2019 at: https://thenewinquiry.com/death-by-twitter/.

Pinder, J. (2012) Online Literary Communities. In Lang, A. (ed.) *From Codex to Hypertext: Reading at the Turn of the Twenty-First Century.* Amherst: University of Massachusetts Press, pp. 68–87.

Pink, S., Horst, H., Postill, J., Hjorth, L., Lewis, T. and Tacchi, J. (2016) *Digital Ethnography.* London: Sage.

Poole, S. (2014) David Mitchell: I've Been Calling *The Bone Clocks* my Midlife Crisis Novel. *The Guardian.* 30 August. Accessed 29 January 2019 at: https://www.theguardian.com/books/2014/aug/30/david-mitchell-interview-bone-clocks-midlife-crisis-novel.

Postill, J. and Pink, S. (2012) Social Media Ethnography: The Digital Researcher in a Messy Web. *Media International Australia*. Nov. (145), pp. 123–134.

Pressman, J. (2014) *Digital Modernism: Making it New in New Media, Modernist Literature & Culture*. New York: Oxford University Press.

Pugh, S. (2005) *The Democratic Genre: Fan Fiction in a Literary Context*. Bridgend: Seren Books.

Rainie, L. and Wellman, B. (2012) *Networked: the New Social Operating System*. Cambridge, MA: MIT Press.

Ray Murray, P. and Squires, C. (2013) The Digital Publishing Communications Circuit. *Book 2.0*. 3. 1, pp. 3–23.

Rettberg, J. Walker (2018) Snapchat: Phatic Communication and Ephemeral Social Media. In Morris, J.W. and Murray, S. (eds) *Appified: Culture in the Age of Apps*. Ann Arbor: University of Michigan Press, pp. 188–196.

Rettberg, S. (2018) *Electronic Literature*. Cambridge: Polity Press.

Rheingold, H. (2000[1993]) *The Virtual Community: Homesteading on the Electronic Frontier*. Cambridge MA: MIT Press.

Rheingold, H. (2017) Netprov: Storytelling as Performing Art. Accessed 1 August 2019 at: https://clalliance.org/blog/netprov-storytelling-performing-art/.

Richards, L. (2000) January Experiences: Martin Amis. *January Magazine*. Accessed 13 August 2019 at: https://www.januarymagazine.com/profiles/amis.html.

Richtel, M. (2008) Introducing the Twiller. *The New York Times*. 29 August. Accessed 17 September 2019 at: https://bits.blogs.nytimes.com/2008/08/29/introducing-the-twiller/.

Rodger, N. (2019) From Bookshelf Porn and Shelfies to #bookfacefriday: How Readers use Pinterest to Promote their Bookishness. *Participations*. 16. 1, pp. 473–495.

Rodley, C. (2015) Magic Realism Bot. Accessed 18 December 2019 at: https://chrisrodley.com/2015/10/10/magic-realism-bot/.

Rogers, R. (2013) Foreword: Debanalising Twitter. In Weller, K., Bruns, A., Burgess, J., Mahrt, M. and Puschmann, C. (eds) *Twitter and Society*. Bern: Peter Lang, pp. ix–xxvi.

Roggenbuck, S., Scott, E.E. and Younghans, R. (2014) *The YOLO Pages*. Online: BoostHouse.

Rowberry, S. (2015) Ebookness. *Convergence*. 23. 3, pp. 289–305.

Rowberry, S. (2016) Commonplacing the Public Domain: Reading the Classics Socially on the Kindle. *Language and Literature*. 25. 3, pp. 211–225.

Sansom, I. (2013) Taipei by Tao Lin – Review. *The Guardian*. July 4. Accessed 29 January 2019 at: https://www.theguardian.com/books/2013/jul/04/taipei-tao-lin-review.

Schwartz, R. and Halegoua, G.R. (2015) The Spatial Self: Location-based Identity Performance on Social Media. *New Media and Society*. 17. 10, pp. 1643–1660.

Scolari, C. (2018) *Teens, Media and Collaborative Cultures*. Accessed 29 January 2019 at: https://repositori.upf.edu/handle/10230/34245.

Scott, S. (2013) Who's Steering the Mothership? The Role of the Fanboy Auteur in Transmedia Storytelling. In Delwiche, A. and Henderson, J.J. (eds) *The Participatory Cultures Handbook*. London: Routledge, pp. 43–50.

Seymour, R. (2019) *The Twittering Machine*. London: Indigo Press.

Shakespeare, S. (2017) Sharp-tongued Salman Rushdie Quits Twitter and Condemns the Social Media Site for Ushering in a 'Generation of Rude People'. *Daily Mail Online*. 29 August. Accessed 8 August 2019 at: https://www.dailymail.co.uk/news/article-4831656/Sharp-tongued-Sir-Salman-Rushdie-quits-Twitter.html.

Skains, L. (2019) *Digital Authorship: Publishing in the Attention Economy*. Cambridge: Cambridge University Press.

Sobieck, B. (2018) *The Writer's Guide to Wattpad*. Writer's Digest Books.

Squires, C. (2007) *Marketing Literature: The Making of Contemporary Writing in Britain*. Basingstoke: Palgrave Macmillan.

Sreedharan, C. (2014) *Epic Retold*. Uttar Pradesh, India: Harper Collins.

Standage, T. (2000) *The Victorian Internet*. London: Phoenix.

Stanfill, M. and Condis, M. (2014) Fandom and/as Labor. *Transformative Works and Cultures*. 15. Accessed 29 January 2019 at: https://journal.transformativeworks.org/index.php/twc/article/view/593/421.

Stein, L. (2016) The Limits of Infinite Scroll: Gifsets and Fanmixes as Evolving Fan Traditions. *Flow*. 25 January. Accessed 29 January 2019 at: https://www.flowjournal.org/2016/01/the-limits-of-infinite-scroll-gifsets-and-fanmixes-as-evolving- f an-traditions/.

Striphas, T. (2010) The Abuses of Literacy: Amazon Kindle and the Right to Read. *Communication and Critical Studies*. 7. 3, pp. 297–317.

Terranova, T. (2000) Free Labor: Producing Culture for the Digital Economy. *Social Text*. 18. 2, pp. 33–58.

Thomas, B. (2007a) Canons and Fanons: Literary Fanfiction Online. *Digital Dichtung*. 37. Accessed 29 January 2019 at: http://www.dichtung-digital.org/2007/thomas.htm.

Thomas, B. (2007b) Stuck in a Loop? Dialogue in Hypertext Fiction. *Narrative*. 15. 3, pp. 357–372.

Thomas, B. (2011a) 'Update Soon!' Harry Potter Fanfiction and Narrative as Participatory Process. In Page, R. and Thomas, B. (eds) *New Narratives: Stories and Storytelling in a Digital Age*. Lincoln, NE: University of Nebraska Press, pp. 205–219.

Thomas, B. (2011b) What is Fanfiction and Why Are People Saying Such Nice Things about It? *Storyworlds*. 3, pp. 1–24.

Thomas, B. (2011c) Trickster Authors and Tricky Readers on the MZD Forums. In Bray, J. and Gibbons, A. (eds) *Mark Z. Danielewski*. Manchester: Manchester University Press, pp. 68–85.

Thomas, B. (2012) *Fictional Dialogue: Speech and Conversation in the Modern and Postmodern Novel*. Lincoln NE: University of Nebraska Press.

Thomas, B. (2014a) 140 Characters in Search of a Story: Twitterfiction as an Emerging Narrative Form. In Bell, A., Ensslin, A. and Rustad, H.K. (eds) *Analysing Digital Fiction*. London: Routledge, pp. 94–108.

Thomas, B. (2014b) Fans Behaving Badly? Real Person Fic and the Blurring of the Boundaries between the Public and the Private. In Thomas, B. and Round, J. *Real Lives, Celebrity Stories: Narratives of Ordinary and Extraordinary People across Media*. London: Bloomsbury, pp. 171–185.

Thomas, B. (2016) Tales from the Timeline: Experiments with Narrative on Twitter. *Comparative Critical Studies*. 13. 3, pp. 353–369.

Thomas, B. (2017) Whose Story is it Anyway? Following Everyday Accounts of Living with Dementia on Social Media. *Style*. 51. 3, pp. 357–373.

Thomas, B. and Round, J. (2012) Research Findings. Accessed 29 January 2019 at: http://www.researchingreadersonline.com/research-findings/.

Thomas, B. and Round, J. (2016) Moderating Readers and Reading Online. *Language and Literature*. 25. 3. 239–253.

Thompson, R. (2018) This Instagram Poet is Making Young People Feel Less Alone. *Mashable UK*. 7 August. Accessed 29 January 2019 at: https://mashable.com/article/instagram-poet-charly-cox/?europe=true.

Todd, R. (1996) *Consuming Fictions: The Booker Prize and Fiction in Britain Today*. London: Bloomsbury.

Tranter, R. (2016) @SamuelBBeckett: Tweets for Everyday Life. *The Score: An Insider's Guide to the Performing Arts*. Accessed 18 August 2019 at: http://www.lincolncenter.org/article/beckett-tweets-for-everyday-life.

Vadde, A. (2017) Amateur Creativity: Contemporary Literature and the Digital Publishing Scene. *New Literary History*. 48. 1, pp. 27–51.

van Dijck, J. (2013) *The Culture of Connectivity: A Critical History of Social Media*. Oxford: Oxford University Press.

van Dijck, J. and Poell, T. (2013) Understanding Social Media Logic. *Media and Communication*. 1. 1, pp. 2–14.

Vecsey, D. (2014) Teju Cole Puts Story-Telling to the Twitter Text. *The New York Times*. 9 January. Accessed 17 August 2019 at: https://6thfloor.blogs.nytimes.com/2014/01/09/teju-cole-puts-story-telling-to-the-twitter-test/.

Vlieghe, J., Page, K. and Rutten, C. (2016) 'Twitter, the most brilliant tough love editor you'll ever have.' Reading and Writing Socially during the Twitter Fiction Festival. *First Monday*, 21. 4. Accessed 29 January 2019 at: https://firstmonday.org/ojs/index.php/fm/article/view/6334/5326.

Vorel, J. (2019) YouTuber Lindsay Ellis Has Been Nominated for a Hugo Award for Her Acclaimed 'Hobbit Duology'. *Paste*. 2 April 2019. Accessed 15 July 2019 at: https://www.pastemagazine.com/articles/2019/04/youtuber-lindsay-ellis-has-been-nominated-for-a-hu.html.

Walker, J. (2004) Distributed Narrative: Telling Stories across Networks. Paper presented at *AoIR 5.0*. Accessed 29 January 2019 at: http://jilltxt.net/txt/AoIR-distributednarrative.pdf.

Wardrip-Fruin, N. (2006) *First Person: New Media as Story, Performance and Game*. Cambridge, MA: MIT Press.

Warfield, K., Cambre, C. and Abidin, C. (2016) Introduction to the Social Media + Society Special Issue on Selfies: Me-diated Inter-faces. *Social Media + Society*. April–June, pp. 1–5.

Wargo, J.M. (2015) 'Every selfie tells a story…' LGBTQ Youth Lifestreams and New Media Narratives as Connective Identity Texts. *New Media and Society.* 19. 4, pp. 560–578.

Watters, C. (2017) #Bookstagram: How Readers Changed the Way We Use Instagram. *Huffington Post.* 26 October. Accessed 29 January 2019 at: https://www.huffingtonpost.com/entry/bookstagram-how-readers-changed-the-way-we-use-in stagram_us_59f0aaa2e4b01ecaf1a3e867.

Watts, R. (2018) The Cult of the Noble Amateur. *PN Review.* 44. 3. Accessed 29 January 2019 at: https://www.pnreview.co.uk/cgi-bin/scribe?item_id=10090.

Weber, M. (2018) *Literary Festivals and Contemporary Book Culture.* Basingstoke: Palgrave Macmillan.

Weedon, A. (2007) In Real Life: Book Covers in the Internet Bookstore. In Moody, N. and Matthews, N. (eds) *Judging a Book by Its Cover: Fans, Publishers, Designers, and the Marketing of Fiction.* London: Ashgate, pp. 117–128.

Weller, K., Bruns, A., Burgess, J., Mahrt, M. and Puschmann, C. (eds) (2013) *Twitter and Society.* Bern: Peter Lang.

White, M. (2017) #Bookstagram: How Readers Changed The Way We Use Instagram. *HuffPost.* 25 October. Accessed 19 November 2019 at: https://www.huffpost.com/entry/bookstagram-how-readers-changed-the-way-we-use-in stagram_b_59f0aaa2e4b01ecaf1a3e867?guccounter=1&guce_referrer=aHR0cH M6Ly93d3cuZ29vZ2xlLmNvbvS8&guce_referrer_sig=AQAAAMtj7PKJIIEX 5omAUJ_wpS8peQC-c5KuqVQCaMMA3bV68jjVBktXfU9GqsjAufgUHAsA dDHKoOZzXYRV2uFoX5DCUgIITdWtFP8nijENuj6aScscV8PmFPEh0xUF Apvxr-IT3A5iW7k_uEwQgQditksCE2cRuDaDNw0uecsMmhys.

Whiteman, N. (2012) *Undoing Ethics: Rethinking Practice in Online Research.* New York: Springer.

Williams, J. (2018) *Stand Out of Our Light: Freedom and Resistance in the Attention Economy.* Cambridge: Cambridge University Press.

Williams, R. (1974) *Television: Technology and Cultural Form.* London: Fontana.

Williams, R. (2018) Tumblr's GIF Culture and the Infinite Image: Lone Fandom, Ruptures, and Working Through on a MICROBLOGGING Platform. *Transformative Works and Cultures.* 27. Accessed 29 January 2019 at: https://journa l.transformativeworks.org/index.php/twc/article/view/1153.

Winterson, J. (2000) *The Powerbook.* London: Jonathan Cape.

Winterson, J. (2001) The Powerbook. Accessed 29 January 2019 at: http://www.jeanettewinterson.com/book/the-powerbook/.

Wittig, R. (2012) Grace, Wit &Charm. Accessed 19 November 2019 at: http://robwit.net/?project=grace-wit-charm.

Wright, T. (2017) Email Interview by Bronwen Thomas.

Yourgrau, B. (2009) Thumb Novels: Mobile Phone Fiction. *The Independent.* 29 July. Accessed 29 January 2019 at: https://www.independent.co.uk/life-style/ga dgets-and-tech/features/thumb-novels-mobile-phone-fiction-1763849.html.

Zappavigna, M. (2011) Ambient Affiliation: A Linguistic Perspective on Twitter. *New Media and Society.* 13. 5, pp. 788–806.

Zappavigna, M. (2014) Ambient Affiliation in Microblogging: Bonding around the Quotidian. *Media International Australia*. 151. 1, pp. 97–103.

Zhang, S. (2013) Teju Cole on the 'Empathy Gap' and Tweeting Drone Strikes. *Mother Jones*. 6 March. Accessed 29 January 2019 at: https://www.mother jones.com/media/2013/03/teju-cole-interview-twitter-drones-small-fates/.

Zubernis, L. and Larsen, K. (2018) Make Space for Us! Fandom in the Real World. In Booth, P. (ed.) *A Companion to Media Fandom and Fan Studies*. London: Wiley, pp. 143–159.

Index

Page numbers in *italics* indicate Figures.

For Product Safety Concerns and Information please contact our EU
representative GPSR@taylorandfrancis.com
Taylor & Francis Verlag GmbH, Kaufingerstraße 24, 80331 München, Germany

* 9 7 8 0 4 1 5 7 8 9 0 9 7 *